Cambridge Elements

Elements in Musical Theatre
edited by
William A. Everett
University of Missouri-Kansas City

THE REBIRTH OF SATIRE IN REVIVALS OF EUROPEAN OPERETTAS

Lisa Feurzeig
Grand Valley State University

Shaftesbury Road, Cambridge CB2 8EA, United Kingdom

One Liberty Plaza, 20th Floor, New York, NY 10006, USA

477 Williamstown Road, Port Melbourne, VIC 3207, Australia

314–321, 3rd Floor, Plot 3, Splendor Forum, Jasola District Centre, New Delhi – 110025, India

103 Penang Road, #05–06/07, Visioncrest Commercial, Singapore 238467

Cambridge University Press is part of Cambridge University Press & Assessment, a department of the University of Cambridge.

We share the University's mission to contribute to society through the pursuit of education, learning and research at the highest international levels of excellence.

www.cambridge.org
Information on this title: www.cambridge.org/9781009571968

DOI: 10.1017/9781009373340

© Lisa Feurzeig 2025

This publication is in copyright. Subject to statutory exception and to the provisions of relevant collective licensing agreements, no reproduction of any part may take place without the written permission of Cambridge University Press & Assessment.

When citing this work, please include a reference to the DOI 10.1017/9781009373340

First published 2025

A catalogue record for this publication is available from the British Library

ISBN 978-1-009-57196-8 Hardback
ISBN 978-1-009-37336-4 Paperback
ISSN 2631-6528 (online)
ISSN 2631-651X (print)

Cambridge University Press & Assessment has no responsibility for the persistence or accuracy of URLs for external or third-party internet websites referred to in this publication and does not guarantee that any content on such websites is, or will remain, accurate or appropriate.

For EU product safety concerns, contact us at Calle de José Abascal, 56, 1°, 28003 Madrid, Spain, or email eugpsr@cambridge.org

The Rebirth of Satire in Revivals of European Operettas

Elements in Musical Theatre

DOI: 10.1017/9781009373340
First published online: June 2025

Lisa Feurzeig
Grand Valley State University

Author for correspondence: Lisa Feurzeig, feurzeil@gvsu.edu

Abstract: Since 1997, revivals have moved operetta away from the nostalgic performance style of the mid twentieth century, returning to its original satirical spirit grounded in ironic mockery of political and social norms and institutions. This Element compares productions of Offenbach's *Belle Hélène* and Kálmán's *Herzogin von Chicago*, considering their choices with regard to plot, text, performance style, music, and costumes and sets. In every case, there is some reinterpretation involved. Satire of times, places, and current politics can be found. Some versions tweak the original while others expand and alter it in a full Regietheater approach, often influenced by a postmodern aesthetic. Directors and performers perceive an opportunity to recreate the central experience of operetta – but is that defined as the original text, Dionysian pleasure, or absurdist theater? The genre lives on mostly through creative approaches to revival.

Keywords: operetta, satire, Regietheater, Offenbach, Kálmán

© Lisa Feurzeig 2025

ISBNs: 9781009571968 (HB), 9781009373364 (PB), 9781009373340 (OC)
ISSNs: 2631-6528 (online), 2631-651X (print)

Contents

1 Operetta's Changing Role and Reputation   1

2 Revivals of Offenbach's *La belle Hélène* between 1994 and 2014   11

3 Revivals of Kálmán's *Die Herzogin von Chicago* in 2004 and 2016   31

4 Operetta Revivals and the Rebirth of Satire   45

    References   52

1 Operetta's Changing Role and Reputation

This study investigates how new productions of old works revitalize and reinterpret the delightful and ironic genre of operetta. The main focus is on six revivals of two important works, one from early in the genre's history, the other toward its final stages. *La belle Hélène* (Beautiful Helen) exemplifies the French style soon after the genre's origins around 1850. One of Offenbach's two anachronistic spoofs of classical mythology, it has remained in the repertoire ever since its 1864 premiere. *Die Herzogin von Chicago* (The Duchess of Chicago), which was created near the end of operetta's heyday, represents the Austro-Hungarian style along with the European fascination with new American sounds in the 1920s. After its 1928 premiere, this work by Emmerich Kálmán was soon categorized as decadent music (*entartete Musik*) by the rising Nazi regime. For that reason, after its early success the work remained in the shadows until its rediscovery in the late 1990s, since which time it has attracted much attention and many performances. The differences between these two works, one established classic of the genre and the other a relative newcomer, make for an interesting comparison of their reinterpretations.

By describing productions of these works from 1994 to 2016, I attempt to analyze the aesthetic and expressive goals of theatrical directors and companies as they return to older works, deciding how to present them to audiences many decades removed from their origins. Although the circumstances of Second Empire France and Central Europe in the 1920s are remote from us in many ways, these works can still charm and excite the public. Temporal distance has encouraged directors, designers, and performers to take many creative approaches, ranging from gentle tweaks of the original to full-blown Regietheater reworkings.

Since operetta's current place in the theatrical world consists primarily of revivals rather than new compositions, it is relevant to ask what the genre signifies now, why it remains on our stages (especially in Europe), and what role it plays. Similar questions apply to other works, such as classic American musicals that continue to have new productions and reinterpretations. Do these works function primarily as a window on the past, a nostalgic revisiting of earlier times? Can revivals and creative new productions make them relevant to our times, just as they were to their own? These are the questions addressed in this study.

What Is Operetta?

What comes to mind when people think of operetta? Many faithful fans would reply that it is an entertaining type of music theater that features lighter music than opera and lots of dancing. Others might mention its sentimental tone, found especially in the Austro-Hungarian repertoire, less so in the flippant French style. Some would emphasize its satirical nature, found for example in the mockery of British institutions by Gilbert and Sullivan: *Iolanthe* took aim at Parliament, *H.M.S. Pinafore* at the military, *Trial by Jury* at the courts, and so on. All these elements are certainly part of the tradition. At the same time, an important characteristic of operetta is that it caters to the tastes and interests of different groups in the audience. Micaela K. Baranello, focusing on Viennese operetta, writes as follows about the genre's hybridity:

> Some of its composers and performers hailed from conservatories and opera houses, others from night clubs and army bands – and many from all of them. They went to the Café Griensteidl and they went to the circus. To write operetta was to stand in the middle of things, to understand high and low and the spaces in between at this confluence of industrialism and early high modernism.... [T]wentieth-century operettas embraced cosmopolitanism, modernity, and sentiment alongside the usual waltzes. They were central to a growing international network of mass entertainment. (Baranello, 2021, p. 2)

Like other genres of music theater, operetta is a multimedia experience that includes text, music, and dance and often features lavish sets and costumes. On top of that, it somehow managed, as Baranello says, to combine modernity and sentiment, two qualities that often seem quite opposed. It is not surprising then, that the experience of a particular theatergoer will depend on that person's background and interests. Operetta appeals to many audiences, and individuals may notice only the elements that they prefer. Many delight in the music, dancing, and luxurious stage sets; others are drawn into the romantic stories; and some appreciate the political and social satire that may range from subtle to glaring. Director Barrie Kosky, whose Offenbach production is discussed in Section 2, recognizes and appreciates this mixed audience. In a 2019 interview, he stated that

> I hate this idea that you do something for a type of audience. I have never understood that.... I wanted my theatre to be full of all sorts of different people [and in Berlin] we have one of the most diverse audiences I've seen anywhere in the world.... such a mixture of students, of grandpas, of queer audience, of operetta fans, people who like musicals, and it's every type and colour and gender and sexuality. And this, for me, is the ideal operetta audience. (Dobesch-Warlick, 2019)

In 2017, when I gave a public lecture in Vienna on operetta as political critique, some attendees indignantly objected, stating that operetta is fun and entertaining, but not political. The strong presence of political references in many operettas makes this outlook seem incomplete – yet it did express the valid experience of those particular spectators. Even so, as Jean-Claude Yon aptly puts it, "the first characteristic of operetta at its origins is the taunting [*raillerie*] of everything that is official, whether it be power or the dominant artistic forms (notably grand opéra)." (Yon, 2007, p. 127. All translations are my own unless otherwise stated.)

Operetta Adaptation and Regietheater

Many modern spectators may not realize that operettas are immensely malleable and that most works have undergone numerous alterations, revisions, and reconceptualizations – not only in recent revivals, but also from their very origin. Operetta scholars are well aware of this, though, and many studies give examples of how quickly new works were adapted and revised as they traveled to other cities and countries. This happened for many reasons. A show might be presented in a smaller or larger theater, leading to new orchestral arrangements or staging decisions. The involvement of particular singer–actors might suggest changing a work to highlight their strengths. Translations into different languages led to inevitable changes in emphasis. If a work included local references, it was logical to adjust those as it moved to different cities. Since operetta was highly commercialized, the idea of *Werktreue* (faithfulness to the original) was less important than popular appeal. Most composers, librettists, and companies were open to making changes, hoping to sell more tickets by matching the taste of a particular community. Theaters presenting operettas generally did not receive the government support that opera theaters did, which increased the incentive to revise.

Even in the classical opera world of the eighteenth and early nineteenth centuries, some changes were viewed as acceptable, such as substitute arias, the ballet Wagner added to *Tannhäuser* for its Paris version, and the significant alteration of the finale of Mozart's *Don Giovanni* when it moved from Prague to Vienna. Operetta lives on the border between classical and popular music and is more governed by the marketplace than opera. Therefore, it is not surprising that during the heyday of the genre, adaptation of operettas to heighten their appeal to a particular community was a completely normal practice.

Regietheater (director's theater) is a term applied to twentieth-century theater and opera productions. It also involves altering the text, music, and/or staging of an original work, but the purpose of those changes is quite different from that just described. In extreme cases, a work can become almost unrecognizable. Ulrich Müller attributes some extreme productions, particularly in Germany, to the existence of government subsidies for the arts: "[a]s a result, the impresarios of these theaters have been only partly dependent on immediate box office success, and have had to struggle increasingly for public attention; in general, it has been worse to be considered old-fashioned than to sell few tickets" (Müller,

2014, p. 588). The resulting productions frequently dismay audiences rather than drawing them to the theaters.

Müller presents Jürgen Kühnel's typology of Regietheater. The types include relatively minor changes, such as staging the work in a time period later than stated in the libretto; symbolic interpretations such as those of Wieland Wagner, who presented his grandfather's music dramas through universalized stage designs emphasizing geometric shapes and light effects; and drastic revisions based on "the staging, not of the story, but of the mental reflexes and reactions of the director" (Müller, 2014, p. 590). In extreme cases, the outcome of the story may be altered. Regietheater productions frequently politicize works from the past by connecting them to more recent historical events, often making references to Fascism and Nazism. Many onlookers are outraged by productions that seem to violate the intentions of a work's original creators.

By contrast, operetta adaptations were often sanctioned and even facilitated by their creators – for example, when Offenbach wrote new material for performances of his works in Berlin. Changes to operettas were normally designed for audience appeal, while Regietheater productions often repel and anger the public – but nevertheless, the degree of change in operetta performances could be quite extreme at times. The following quotations illustrate the procedures and some examples.

Writing about Viennese operettas of the twentieth century, Baranello describes the production materials that were sent to new theaters after a work's premiere:

> the final version of the text was printed as a *Regie- und Soufflierbuch* (direction and prompt book) or *Vollständiges Soufflierbuch mit sämtlichen Regiebemerkungen* (full prompt book with complete production notes).... The original staging was considered an integral part of the work ... [b]ut it is clear that for foreign stages directors adapted works for local taste and resources.... Printed librettos and staging manuals should not be considered definitive records of any production. (Baranello, 2020, p. 197)

This normal practice of adapting operetta productions was changed in later Broadway shows, as explained by Anastasia Belina and Derek B. Scott:

> A change in the mid-1980s, initiated by the success of *Phantom of the Opera*, was the desire to see the same production in one city as in another, but in the period this book deals with [mid-nineteenth to mid-twentieth century], productions could vary from city to city, and even their titles changed. To give two examples, Leo Fall's *Der liebe Augustin* became *Princess Caprice* in London, and Eduard Künneke's *Der Vetter aus Dingsda* became *Caroline* in New York. (Belina & Scott, 2020, p. 7)

While Belina and Scott mention *Phantom of the Opera*, even as early as the 1940s, Rodgers and Hammerstein "insisted on replica productions of their works when they were revived."[1] It can be fruitful to compare performance practices for operetta and musical, particularly as some theaters alternate productions of the two. As one example, the leadership of Marcel Prawy led the Vienna Volksoper to include musicals in its repertoire, beginning with *Kiss Me, Kate* in 1956 (Wagner-Trenkwitz, 2022).

The next quotations describe specific productions, starting with cases where changes were governed by audience preferences and moving into others that suggest Regietheater. Veerle Driessen explains how one aria in Offenbach's *Orpheus in der Unterwelt* was altered for an 1867 performance in Amsterdam. In the original, the deceased Hans Styx, wooing Eurydice, sings about his former life on earth as a king. By contrast, in the Amsterdam version

> he did not sing about how Eurydice would have become his wife, but about how, if he were still prince of Arcadia, he would travel with her to Amsterdam and stay there at the then brand new *Amstel Hotel*, stroll along the famous *Kalverstraat*, the most famous shopping street of Amsterdam, and would be enjoying himself in Van Lier's theater. The aria was thus completely adapted to the experience of Amsterdam theatergoers (Driessen, 2023).[2]

Laurence Senelick's book on Offenbach productions all over the world overflows with descriptions of how the works were altered. As one example among many, Senelick discusses Offenbach performances in Japan by touring French and English companies in the late nineteenth century. *La Grande-Duchesse de Gérolstein*, renamed *General Boum*, was a favorite. He writes that "[t]he operas were played for low comedy and cheap melodrama, interspersed with specialty acts and assimilated to Japanese habits whenever possible" (Senelick, 2017, p. 197).

Fall's operetta *Die Dollarprinzessin* had its premiere in Vienna in 1907. Stefan Frey describes its arrival in New York two years later:

> As with everywhere else, it was the Viennese elements that captured the audience of *The Dollar Princess* at its Broadway debut. To counterbalance this 'global' impact, interpolations by domestic composers were usually added. In Fall's operetta, it was for instance the hornpipe quintet 'A Boat Sails on Wednesday' by the as-yet-unknown Jerome Kern . . . (Frey, 2020, p. 90)

---

[1] Everett, W. (2024). Personal communication, 7 June.
[2] This instance of self-referentiality – mentioning the specific theater where a performance is occurring – is similar to one in the 1822 Viennese Volkstheater play *Aline, oder Wien in einem anderen Weltheile* (Aline, or Vienna on Another Continent) by Adolf Bäuerle with music by Wenzel Müller. In this work, the second couple sing a duet about Vienna, also ending with a reference to the very theater where the play was performed: "Was jetzt im Leopoldstädter Theater vorgeht? / Da singt just die Zilly mit dem Bims ein Duett." (What is happening now in the Leopoldstadt Theater? Zilly and Bims are singing a duet there.) See Feurzeig (2014, pp. 162–6).

It was quite normal for new songs to be added in this way when a production traveled to another country – yet how interesting to see the name of such a renowned American composer at the early stages of his career, and eighteen years before *Show Boat*!

In a notable article on operetta performance practice, Kevin Clarke describes jazz versions of Franz Lehár's *Die lustige Witwe*, Kálmán's *Csárdásfürstin*, and other twentieth-century works. For example, "Millöcker's *Dubarry* was arranged by Theo Mackeben (the director of the premiere of the *Dreigroschenoper*) and transformed into a sensational modern success" (Clarke, 2006, p. 43).

Some changes to operetta, such as jazz versions of older works, were designed to attract audiences by keeping up with changing musical taste. From the 1930s onward, though, there were also ideological reasons, since Nazi, Fascist, and Communist governments often required productions and newly written works to conform with their political goals and ideals. This could lead to drastic changes in plot and music. Péter Bozó describes a rewriting of Offenbach's *Grande-Duchesse de Gérolstein* for a performance in Budapest in 1950 in which the plot was redesigned to criticize the Marshall Plan. Even after making these major changes, the theater director, Margit Gáspár, wrote a self-abasing letter to Mátyás Rákosi, the head of state at that time, describing her "serious inner crisis," asking whether the adapted version was "a Communist work or a counter-revolutionary activity," and volunteering that she should be dismissed from her position if she had erred (Bozó, 2022, pp. 49–67; quote from p. 64).

A related example from the Nazi era was the regime's attempts in 1943–44 to rewrite Lehár's 1902 operetta *Der Rastelbinder*, whose original main character was Jewish. In his archival study of letters among government officials, publishers, Lehár, and the adapter Rudolf Weys – whose wife, like Lehár's, was Jewish – Wolfgang Dosch demonstrates that some elements of the original content were preserved despite the political pressures of the situation, and that Lehár saw this project as an opportunity to protect the Weys family (Dosch, 2020).

Political circumstances like these led to very different results than earlier adaptations designed simply to appeal to local audiences. Yet even when a regime had taken one official position – for example, the Nazi aversion to jazz influence on European music – exceptions could be made. For example, as Matthias Kauffmann describes, Fritz Fischer (1898–1985), director of the Gärtnerplatz Theater in Munich from 1938 to 1945, made alterations that incorporated jazz in very pleasurable and often erotic reworkings of older operettas.

> Usually, for no significant reason, he split the original operettas into thirty-three scenes, something that was to become his trademark. Those scenes were altered significantly, and the structure of the original plots was not strictly followed.... In 1939, for instance, *Die Fledermaus* was 'arranged in 33 bouquets' (*Sträusse!*): the first scene was set in heaven, where Fischer's superstar Johannes Heesters, dressed as an immortal Johann Strauss, conducted a heavenly orchestra, playing the famous overture. Fischer did not hesitate to give that orchestra a very jazzy sound... (Kauffmann, 2020, p. 268)

As a final set of examples outside of totalitarian political regimes, performances of the Gilbert and Sullivan operettas range from very traditional to extremely innovative. Performance style for the "Savoy operas" by this famous duo was dominated for decades by the tradition-bound D'Oyly Carte Company, which held the copyright until it expired in 1961. Even so, as Ian Bradley observes, "there was a cross-dressed *Pinafore* as early as 1888, and in 1939 New Yorkers had a choice of 'Swing', 'Hot', or 'Red' versions of the *Mikado*" (Bradley, 2005, p. 168). There was also a notable increase in adapted versions, first after the copyright for the shows expired and again when the D'Oyly Carte Company ceased its operations in 1982. (A new version of that company then came into existence in 1988 and continued till 2003; see Bradley 2005 for more details.)

Even secondary schools sometimes make startling changes when performing Gilbert and Sullivan, as shown by this brief characterization of several productions at St. Mary's Catholic High School near Manchester:

> *Mikado* was transferred to a Nissan car plant in Sunderland to show the Japanese takeover of British industry; *Iolanthe* was performed on roller skates with an Alice in Wonderland theme; and *Yeomen* was set in Blackpool Tower, *Gondoliers* in modern Venice, and *Ruddigore* in 1930s Hollywood. (Bradley, 2005, p. 148)

These St. Mary's productions clearly qualify as Regietheater, since they changed the times and settings and in the case of *The Mikado*, also made the connection of the original Japanese location to a very up-to-date social concern about Japanese business in the United Kingdom. As Regietheater, they exemplify a trend that we will see reflected in several of the productions discussed in the two case studies following this section.

The two types of adaptation described belong essentially to different eras of operetta. Adjusting a work to suit particular circumstances (the theater space, the locale, and the audience) was most natural at the time that operetta was a current genre, with new works continually being composed and circulated. The interpretation-heavy Regietheater approach, while not completely absent in earlier times, was applied to operettas as this form of light opera was becoming a historical genre. Similar reinterpretations of musicals have also begun in recent years: examples include director Daniel Fish's revival of *Oklahoma!* and the very new David Herskovits adaptation of *Show Boat* (Preston, 2021; Green, 2025). But when and why did operetta's shift from a current to a historical genre take place?

From Critique to Nostalgia: World Wars Bring Changes to Operetta

This shift during the first half of the twentieth century is closely correlated with the two world wars and the realignments of European lives, politics, and governmental systems that came with them. Before World War I, many new operettas were still being composed and adapted to suit various theaters and audiences in Central Europe and North America. By the 1950s, the focus of musical theater had shifted away from operetta to the musical. Operetta was viewed as an older art form and its best-known works were canonized, much as the classical music world went through the process of reifying music by Bach, Mozart, and Beethoven. Popular music always moves in new directions as fashions change, but operetta was especially susceptible to this alteration because its ironic outlook depended on the social circumstances of its origins.

In the final chapter of his remarkable study of Viennese operetta, cultural historian Moritz Csáky explains that the dissolution of the Austro-Hungarian Empire after World War I undermined the function and relevance of the old type of Viennese operetta.

> Increasingly, the messages and points [of operetta] were no longer understood; thus, it gradually had to be flattened out into pure nostalgia ... [T]he world of the Monarchy ... from which they were politically distanced, was not only offered up in a guise that called back this past, but was also performed in a consciously nostalgic-kitschy and exaggeratedly ridiculous manner ... But that meant that one of the most essential characteristics of turn-of-the century operetta, humor, was mocked by a change of meaning. For operetta could not mock and ironize a time and society which no longer existed.... With that, Viennese modern operetta lost not only its original function, but also in a certain sense its very justification for existing. (Csáky, 1998, pp. 291–2)

While the Viennese tradition was particularly affected by the Empire's dissolution in 1918, it is evident that similar situations obtained for operetta in other countries, as the genre was usually designed to satirize the present-day situation of its own time. Offenbach's ironic take on Second Empire French society and Gilbert and Sullivan's satire of Victorian England also became outdated under the new circumstances of the early twentieth century, which had its own situations and problems to address. World War I began a process of change in the fundamental structures of European life that accelerated between the wars, and World War II intensified the damage. Both physically and metaphorically, it was necessary to rebuild, and many older traditions were lost in that process.

Despite the turmoil, new operettas continued to be created and produced in Central Europe well into the 1930s, with some notable changes in style. Jazz music and dance were emphasized, and many new works were revue operettas, more focused on presenting interesting and varied music and dance numbers than on coherent plot development. In the Soviet orbit, new operettas that furthered Communist and Socialist ideas – including actual tractor romances, as in Soviet film – were composed well into the 1960s (Belina, 2020b).

Some of the new operettas moved the genre into the present, addressing contemporary issues such as factory work, team sports, and the film industry. This began even before World War I: Fall's 1907 *Die Dollarprinzessin* includes a female chorus of typists, including the sound of their typewriters as part of the music, and the heroine of Lehár's 1911 operetta *Eva* works in a glass factory (Baranello, 2021, pp. 64–72). In a different direction, Paul Abraham's *Die Blume von Hawaii* (The Flower of Hawaii, 1931) addressed American colonialism while also capitalizing on an attractive exotic locale; his *Roxy und ihr Wunderteam* (Roxy and her Magical Team, 1937), first performed in Budapest, is about men's and women's sports. In Ralph Benatzky's *Axel an der Himmelstür* (Axel at the Gates of Heaven, 1936) a young Austrian reporter in Hollywood becomes romantically involved with a Greta-Garbo-like star.[3]

Another creative response was to write new works that capitalized on nostalgia. This can be found in pieces such as Fall's *Die Kaiserin* (The Empress, 1916), a romanticized account of the young Empress Maria Theresia of Austria, and *Madame Pompadour* (1922), a sassy and erotic portrayal of the famous mistress of Louis XV – each designed to showcase the star Fritzi Massary as its title character. Kálmán also emphasized past glories in *Gräfin Mariza* (Countess Maritza, 1924), which is set in prewar Hungary but captured postwar regret.

Nazi cultural policies had a strong effect on operetta, not only before and during World War II but also on the later public image of the genre. Scholars have gathered various types of evidence to document this influence. By examining the gaps in Nazi operetta guides, Volker Klotz demonstrates how the Nazi

---

[3] This operetta was revived by the Vienna Volksoper in 2016, directed by Peter Lund, with clever video projections designed by Andreas Ivancsics. Both Axel and Hollywood star Gloria Mills were played by performers known for their work in musicals, Andreas Bieber and Bettina Mönch, in a successful and friendly collaboration with Volksoper regulars from the operetta and opera world, as I was able to observe in watching rehearsals and performances.

leaders "cleansed" the repertoire by eliminating works created by Jewish composers and librettists (a very large number) and those that emphasized jazz. They also Germanized the genre by minimizing the importance of its French origins and ignoring works from outside Germany and Austria; commissioned substitute works suspiciously close in plot to some of those they had removed; and privileged works that glorified authority and power rather than undermining them through mockery (Klotz, 2014, pp. 85–97).

Based on a close study of the Third Reich's policies and documents compared to the operettas that were actually produced, Matthias Kauffmann argues that the effects of the policies were inconsistent. He describes a "system of pragmatism and double moral standards" that did not live up to its own rhetoric. For example, Goebbels decided to suppress the information that Johann Strauss had one-eighth Jewish heritage, because he felt Strauss's operettas were too important to eliminate (Kauffmann, 2020, pp. 262–3). Despite the regime's supposed rejection of jazz and revue-operetta, in reality both were permitted, as in the Fischer *Fledermaus* production described under Operetta Adaptation and Regietheater, which included "nude stars climb[ing] out of giant champagne glasses" (Kauffmann, 2020, p. 267). Kauffmann describes the mix of earnest works displaying Aryan nationalism with more frivolous productions that appealed to typical audiences, and he concludes that "the Nazis actually did not have the power to kill the genre, but they let it die" (Kauffmann, 2020, p. 270).

Kevin Clarke uses historical recordings to trace shifts in operetta performance style, stating that the influence of Nazi preferences led to "a performance practice that has created for the genre, since the Second World War, the worst image one could imagine." He argues that the shift from singer–actors who performed in cabaret style to operatic voices brought excessive sentimentality that snuffed out the campiness, ironic humor, and overt eroticism of the original works (Clarke, 2006, p. 24). At the end of this article, Clarke expresses his scornful appraisal of the outdoor summer performances in Mörbisch, Austria: "Little can be found in Mörbisch of the original *Maritza*'s glamorous 20s flair, since this Burgenland festival presents Kálmán and all operetta as extremely stale [*altbacken*], folkloric, and of yesterday – for an elderly public that wants to see a live *Heimatfilm*"[4] (Clarke, 2006, p. 63).

With this term, Clarke is referring to a type of nostalgic film that was popular in Germany and Austria after World War II; a subset of these movies were

---

[4] While Clarke's overall point is well-taken, I would like to defend this particular Mörbisch production. I used it in a class on music and humor, and I believe it was very effective in conveying the style of 1920s operetta to students who were far from elderly. Also, it is worth mentioning that the altered dialogue sometimes refers to current political topics, as for example when Mariza and Zsupán, comparing the size of their pig herds, mention EU regulations.

operetta adaptations or newly composed operettas for film. They frequently (though not always) presented a more buttoned-up and less risqué version of the genre that matched operetta's role as an expression of nostalgia. Derek B. Scott discusses *Heimat* films, which "had a nostalgic appeal in their emphasis on wholesome and supposedly traditional values lived by honest folk overcoming adversity in idyllic rural locations." As a related example, he discusses the 1952 and 1960 film versions of Benatzky's 1930 operetta *Im weißen Rössl*, pointing out that irony was gradually eliminated, so that "in the 1960 film directed by Werner Jacobs, all traces of the frivolity, mischief, camp and caricature of [director Erik] Charell's original revue operetta – the features that lent it a tone of social critique – had vanished" (Scott, 2020, pp. 281–2).

Operetta's original role as a critique and send-up of social norms and institutions was largely lost, and there was much less of a reason to compose new works in the genre. Instead, since 1945 the theatrical world of Western Europe and North America has come to treat operetta as a known quantity and an opportunity for revivals. As with opera, there is a standard repertoire of favorites that are produced over and over, while lesser-known operettas are occasionally brought out of the shadows and into the spotlight. The works discussed in the next two sections of this Element include one of each.

Csáky mentions a "rediscovery or revaluation" of operetta beginning in the 1980s and suggests that the Viennese repertoire of the genre might "reach [*den Bogen spannen*] into the present and perhaps facilitate our understanding ... of our own multipolar identity" (Csáky, 1998, p. 300). My broad question in the two case studies that follow is whether recent revivals and new productions of older operettas continue to function as a venue for sentimentalism and nostalgia, or whether eroticism, campiness, and social-political critique are returning to the operetta stage. In the past, these vital characteristics of the genre were expressed through the creation of new works. Is it possible that these thrilling qualities are now found instead in creative revivals?

2 Revivals of Offenbach's *La belle Hélène* between 1994 and 2014

Jacques Offenbach is widely recognized as the composer whose works defined the operetta genre as it was taking shape. He wrote over 100 theatrical works, of which some, such as *Barbe-bleue* (Bluebeard, 1866) set fairy tales and legends while others, such as *La Vie parisienne* (Parisian Life, 1866) and *La Grande-Duchesse de Gérolstein* (The Grand Duchess of Gérolstein, 1867) depicted modern European life. Within his varied oeuvre, two of his most significant and memorable works were set in the world of classical antiquity. Under the guise of retelling classical myths, these satirical works overflowed with obvious references to the circumstances and inconsistencies of contemporary European society. For example, rather than emphasizing faithful love within marriage – the tradition in Orpheus operas since Monteverdi – *Orphée aux enfers* (Orpheus in the Underworld, 1858) portrayed Orpheus and Eurydice as a dissatisfied couple who are delighted that the snake's deadly bite offers them the opportunity to end their marriage. Their choices are somewhat curbed only to avoid provoking the censorious character personified as Public Opinion.

The work discussed here, *La belle Hélène,* is similarly snarky and irreverent in its revision of the mythical story. I believe this helps explain its many revivals in the late twentieth and early twenty-first centuries, when the function of operetta as a vehicle for social commentary and criticism was coming back into fashion. This work – undeniably clever, amusing, and entertaining in both story and music – has inspired numerous reinterpretations, four of which are discussed in this section.

Well before the productions discussed here, though, this highly popular operetta had been presented in many forms, with changes to the original ranging from minor adjustments to extensive reworkings. Herbert Schneider has done extensive research on some of these, emphasizing what he describes as the "six most important German versions" between 1865 and 2008. He provides extensive detail on cuts to the music, changes to the text, and added material in these. The most heavily revised version he describes, from 1931, was directed by Max Reinhardt and included new music by Erich Wolfgang Korngold and texts by Egon Friedell and Hans Sassman. Schneider's tallies of that production reveal that "eleven of Offenbach's pieces are removed, six uncut and six cut, and thirty-two pieces are new"! (Schneider, 2020, pp. 24, 28) That version was produced in theaters in Berlin and Vienna.

I begin with an overview of the work and some of its notable elements. After that, I discuss each of the four productions with attention to staging decisions and any notable alterations to the original. These productions took place in Zurich in 1994, Paris in 2000, and Hamburg and Berlin in 2014. For more details, see Table 1. Given the limitations of space, I have chosen to describe one scene that particularly characterizes each production. In addition, I compare each production's approach to the scene in Act II when Paris and Helen become physically intimate.

Synopsis of *La belle Hélène*

The story, set at the Spartan court, represents the events leading up to the Trojan War. (I use the English character names rather than the French.) Helen, the queen, is shown to be a dissatisfied wife who has had many affairs that she attributes to Fate ("la fatalité!"), seeing them as inevitable since she herself is the offspring of Leda's adulterous union with Jupiter when he took the shape of a swan. Her husband is portrayed as a weak and unattractive figure; his entrance lines are "I am the husband of the queen, King Menelaus." This is mythologically accurate, as Helen was a Spartan princess, so the kingship came with marriage to her – but this self-deprecating phrase also expresses her dominance in their marriage. Their nephew Orestes, played as a pants role, is a frivolous young man who greatly enjoys nightlife, using tax money to pursue his pleasures. Another significant character is Calchas, priest of Jupiter, who laments the decline of religion in public life.

In Act I, Paris of Troy arrives dressed as a shepherd, not long after his fateful encounter with the three goddesses. Calchas, who has already heard about this, asks him to describe the beauties of Venus, which he does in a lascivious suggestive way. After receiving a letter purportedly from Venus herself, Calchas becomes Paris's ally in his quest to seduce Helen. Next comes a festival of religious sacrifice, attended by several other Greek kings. They take part in a kind of intellectual triathlon that includes a game of charades, whose solution is the word "locomotive" (a perfect example of the anachronisms at the center of this drama) – and the unknown young shepherd wins, surprising everyone with his brilliance. He then reveals that he is not just a shepherd, but Paris, Prince of Troy, which leads to a delightful ensemble in which he is greeted as "the man with the apple" which charmingly rhymes in French: "l'homme à la pomme." As Hans-Jörg Neuschäfer points out, a key element in this work is that the characters have some foreknowledge of the mythical events; thus, everyone has already heard about the "Judgement of Paris" (Neuschäfer, 1985, p. 124). Menelaus invites Paris to join the court for dinner that evening, but Calchas contrives a prophecy commanding Menelaus to spend a month in the mountains of Crete, and he departs immediately, shooed away by a cheerful chorus despite the general awareness that this journey threatens his marriage.

Helen is attracted to Paris but strives to protect her virtue. At the same time, she is keenly aware that she truly has no choice, as Venus has promised her to Paris (that foreknowledge again). Act II shows her preparing for dinner about a month later, rejecting her attendants' suggestion that she wear a low-cut dress. She sings an aria, reproaching Venus for putting both her and her mother in situations where they must betray their marriage vows. The kings, still visiting Sparta, play a gambling game called "the game of the goose" that Calchas wins by cheating. Eventually, Helen decides not to attend the dinner. Wishing to keep Paris in the realm of fantasy, she asks Calchas to send her a dream about him. Paris enters her room disguised as a slave. Emboldened by the belief that she is dreaming, Helen asks him to compare her beauty with that of Venus; he uses this as an opportunity to encourage her to uncover her body, and they become physically intimate. Helen continues to believe (or persuade herself) that the encounter is a dream – until Menelaus suddenly enters, having left Crete early. He indignantly awakens the court, calling the other kings to witness his wife's infidelity. Helen declares, to general agreement, that a husband should never return from a journey without informing his wife. If she knows in advance, she can perform the necessary cover-up to protect everyone's honor and reputation. In this act, it is Paris who is shooed away, this time by an indignant chorus.

As Act III begins, we learn that Venus, enraged that her plans are being thwarted, has made all the people of Greece sex-crazy, leading to complete turmoil as wives and husbands abandon one another. Menelaus is still angry at Helen and demands that she explain her comment that what happened between her and Paris was only a dream; she responds petulantly to his pestering. Agamemnon and Calchas try to persuade Menelaus to sacrifice his personal happiness for the welfare of his subjects by appeasing Venus's anger, and he replies that he has already invited her high priest to come and resolve the situation. The impending arrival of a competing high priest arouses the professional jealousy of Calchas. When this priest (actually Paris) arrives on a special boat, he first admonishes the Spartans to stop their mournful singing and be happy; this is the well-known Tyrolienne, complete with flashy yodeling for Paris. He proclaims that to satisfy Venus, Helen must accompany him on a brief penitential journey to the island of Cythera, which is sacred to Venus. Helen resists until the priest quietly reveals his identity. The two of them sail away as the "high priest" mocks Menelaus, revealing that he is Paris and Helen will not be returning. The final chorus is set to the same music as the end of Act I. Just as the ensemble had sent Menelaus off to Crete, they now shoo Helen and Paris off to Cythera. The libretto includes an additional verse in which they express anger and predict the war to come, but this part of the text is frequently omitted, so that the ending becomes a celebration of love and infidelity.

Social Critique, Anachronism, Intertextuality, and Musical Reference in the Original Work

As we know, operetta was a satirical genre, usually including parody of musical traditions, references to other musical and literary works, and mockery of social norms and institutions. *La belle Hélène* is a textbook example of these tendencies. Beyond the expected use of parody, a work set in classical antiquity offers many opportunities for anachronistic references to much later times in both text and music, and the librettists and composer of *La belle Hélène* took full advantage of this source of humor. These elements – social critique, intertextual reference, musical parody, and anachronism – are closely intertwined, so it is logical to discuss them together rather than tease them apart.

The work's portrayal of mythological Greek kings and heroes as self-aggrandizing, silly, and hedonistic takes some of the larger themes of the *Iliad* to extremes and was perceived by contemporary audience members as shocking and even blasphemous. Prince Richard von Metternich, the Austrian Ambassador to France, attended the premiere with his wife and remarked afterward that they would be mentioned in the newspapers, and that it was not agreeable for a lady to be associated with such a scandalous work (Fraison, 1989, p. 16). Helen is depicted as driven by circumstances beyond her control, which she frequently apostrophizes as "la fatalité," yet she also takes advantage of this circumstance, which provides an excuse for her to enjoy the developing affair with Paris and her eventual abduction. As mentioned earlier, Neuschäfer observes that the operetta alters the presentation of the story in an important way.

> The trick of the reference to the myth consists in the fact that Offenbach and Meilhac/Halévy furnish their characters with a quantum of foreknowledge of their story. As a result, first of all the characters can hardly be surprised by its unfolding, and secondly they are unburdened of responsibility and have a certain leeway [*Spielraum*] to choose frivolous options. (Neuschäfer, 1985, p. 124.)

Textual anachronism is most notable in the Act I game of charades, which Paris wins with the correct answer "locomotive." There is a later reference to a train departing in Act III. When a dove arrives bringing the letter from Venus, Calchas carefully removes the stamp for the collection of Princess Hermione. Musical anachronism is omnipresent, as the music is of its own time, not at all related to anything ancient Greek. Naturally, the operetta audience would not expect ancient music, but nevertheless, the presence of familiar nineteenth-century genres of entertainment music such as polka, waltz, and Tyrolienne adds absurd humor, supporting the anachronisms in the text.

Other scholars have noted that Offenbach uses direct and implied quotations from other operas. Many details can be found in David Rissin's commentary on the libretto. For example, he points out a resemblance between a phrase of Helen's opening air sung to Venus and Susanna's recitative at the end of Mozart's

Marriage of Figaro; both passages involve a woman expressing her need for or anticipation of love. The most notable case of direct quotation is heard in the Act III trio, whose first line exactly quotes the music of a trio in Act II of Rossini's *Guillaume Tell*. This is an apt reference, as the situations are quite parallel. In the Rossini example, two friends attempt to persuade Arnold to renounce his romantic involvement with the Habsburg princess Mathilde and join the Swiss rebellion. In the Offenbach example, two friends advise Menelaus to set aside his personal wishes regarding his marriage to do what is necessary for the country (Rissin, 1989, pp. 29, 77–79).

Along with quotations from specific works, grand opera is satirized through stylistic allusions, some written by Offenbach and some added by performers. A strong example from Offenbach's score is the elaborate florid writing on the words "Ô ciel! L'homme à la pomme!" (O heavens! The man with the apple!) in the Act I Finale, sung first by Helen and then passed around the ensemble. By contrast, Helen's exclamation at the end of Act III, "C'est encore la fatalité!" (It is fate once again!) is written simply in the score, with a fermata over her high F on the syllable "ta" – but at least in modern performances, it is expected that the singer will add extensive ornaments here. The most extreme example I encountered was in the Hamburg production; Jennifer Larmore's version of this phrase is explained in the description of that production.

Mockery of French social norms is evident in the representation of marriage customs, upper-class society, religion, and government spending. The libretto makes it completely clear that marriage is neither viewed as sacred nor based on love. Helen states that she cannot love her husband and is trying to be virtuous purely to meet social expectations; almost everyone around her takes her infidelities with Paris and her previous history with other men in a light and humorous spirit. Commentators on this operetta agree that this reflects the behavior of French high society in the Second Empire. The elite class is portrayed as extremely silly, with the kings and high priests partaking in party games and frolicking on the beach. Calchas, the symbol of organized religion, cheats at cards and has a machine that produces fake thunder, which he uses whenever he needs to announce a message "from Jupiter," though he actually contrives these messages himself. Finally, the libretto emphasizes the royals' use of public money to finance their personal expenses. Orestes mentions in his opening aria that Agamemnon does not mind funding his son's hedonistic pleasures because Greece will pay. Upon being told that Venus requires the sacrifice of one hundred white cows, Menelaus similarly states that his people will pay the costs. This clearly satirizes taxation policy and social inequality in nineteenth-century Europe rather than the governmental structure of ancient Greece.

Four Productions

Table 1 lists the four productions discussed here and their directing teams.

As we examine these versions, some questions arise that would present themselves to any creative team deciding how to approach this work.

- In what time period(s) is the production set?
- What visual style(s) and references are included?
- How much anachronism is used, and in what forms?
- How to represent the most beautiful woman in the world – should this be done straight or ironically?
- How far to go in the bedroom scene?
- Is the purpose of this production to reproduce the original show as faithfully as possible, or to add new interpretations and references?

Each production resolves these questions differently. Broadly speaking, the Paris and Hamburg productions are the most similar, yet each has its own individuality. I do not discuss the details of how the spoken dialogue is altered; the original libretto has a great deal of it, and each production makes some cuts and adaptations. To go beyond that generalization would shift the goal of this section, which is to capture the essential qualities of the productions through descriptive writing, not to catalogue every deviation from the original. I address the productions in chronological order.

Table 1 Productions of *La belle Hélène*

Company	Year	Conductor	Stage director	Sets/Costumes
Zurich Opera	1994 (DVD 1997)	Nikolaus Harnoncourt	Helmuth Lohner	Paolo Piva/ Jean-Charles de Castelbajac
Théâtre du Châtelet (Paris)	2000 (DVD 2002)	Marc Minkowski	Laurent Pelly	Chantal Thomas /Laurent Pelly
Hamburg Staatsoper	2014	Gerrit Priessnitz	Renaud Doucet	André Barbe
Berlin Komische Oper	2014	Henrik Nánási	Barrie Kosky	Rufus Didwiszus/ Buki Schiff

Zurich 1994

The Zurich production hews most closely to the original, though it certainly adds idiosyncratic whimsy and charm. A major contributor to that spirit is conductor Nikolaus Harnoncourt, who had worked closely with the Zurich Opera since 1975. His first projects there were cycles of Monteverdi and Mozart collaborating with stage director Jean-Pierre Ponnelle. His first venture into operetta in Zurich was Strauss's *Der Zigeunerbaron* in 1990; *La belle Hélène* followed in 1994, and the video was released in 1997 (Gutknecht, 2009). Renowned as a champion of historically informed performance, Harnoncourt helped to move this approach from its original territory of music of the Baroque and Classical eras into the nineteenth century. His delight in performing operetta is evident, and the light, quick touch that he brings to the orchestral tone is effective. The DVD shows him occasionally singing along in the pit, and there are charming moments when Helen interacts directly with him, once addressing him as "Maestro."

The set is modeled on the Roman Pantheon, depicting the inside of the famous dome rising high at the back of the stage, as though the performers are all inside the building. This set is present throughout, even for Act III, which takes place at the beach. Many of the costumes also reference older styles, but in an eclectic mix that ranges from tunics and togas for male characters to more recent dress styles for Helen. The costumes were designed by Jean-Charles de Castelbajac, who works primarily in the world of fashion – he is currently the artistic director of the Benetton Group and has dressed pop stars including Madonna, Lady Gaga, Beyoncé, and Drake (Stephinson, 2023). Costume designer Cat O'Callaghan describes his overall approach in *La belle Hélène* as "a stylized fusion of modern and historical fashion."[5]

Notably, many costumes have words written on them in French, Latin, or English. On Helen's hoop-skirted ballgown in Act I, the word "L'AMOUR" is inscribed in red letters, probably made of dyed feathers stitched onto the skirt. (Film director Baz Luhrmann is known for his insertion of a neon "L'Amour" sign, for example, in *Romeo and Juliet* (1996) and *Moulin Rouge!* (2001) – which may be linked to the whole set of *Hélène* productions, as Luhrmann and Barrie Kosky of the Berlin production were both young Australians directing operas in the 1980s and 1990s.) Figure 1 shows this costume.

When Paris makes his first appearance, his tunic contains the text of a mock classified ad in French: "I seek the most beautiful woman in the world . . . " and

---

[5] O'Callaghan, C. (2023). Personal communication about costumes in Zurich production of *La belle Hélène*, September 6.

Figure 1 Vesselina Kasarova in her grand "L'AMOUR" dress. Photo reproduced with the permission of the Opernhaus Zürich and Peter Schlegel.

includes his phone number, extending the anachronisms of the nineteenth-century original work. The chorus members wear similar outfits that O'Callaghan describes as a style influenced by ancient Greek and Roman tunics. These are also inscribed with schematic drawings and words in various languages: for example, one depicts a large human hand with the words "la main de la fatalité" (the hand of fate), while others have depictions of a spiral maze, a head wearing a crown, and a fish standing on its tail below a crown. Others feature words such as "lux," "pax," "U. F. O.," "cloud," "angel," and "dream." As performers move around the stage, these texts are not fully seen or easily read, making them all the more enticing to spectators. These inscribed costumes both

Figure 2 Helen with chorus members, showing Pantheon set and inscribed costumes. Photo reproduced with the permission of the Opernhaus Zürich and Peter Schlegel.

evoke and mock the deeper levels of the myth while highlighting connections of the ancient Greek legend with archetypes and symbols of other civilizations, such as ancient Egypt and biblical Christianity. Figure 2 shows some of these inscribed costumes and also gives a good sense of the Pantheon set.

The performer playing Helen is Bulgarian mezzo-soprano Vesselina Kasarova, who was about twenty-nine at the time of the production. Her costumes and makeup accentuate her youth and traditional beauty, making her believable as the legendary Helen. I mention this not to rank her appearance against that of other performers, but to point out that this casting choice seems to be a conscious strategy of the directing team, quite different from the choices made in some other productions.

Another point of comparison among the productions is how they represent the events taking place during the love duet (perhaps better labeled as the adultery duet), Act II, Scene X. In this number, Helen persuades herself that the presence of Paris in her room at night is a dream, and he goes along with her belief, taking his opportunity to become intimate with her. She asks him to compare her beauty with that of Venus; he persuades her to be more open by hinting that beauty is as beauty does and encouraging her to emulate Venus by showing her body and kissing him. In the Zurich production (whose Paris was Deon van der Walt), the two performers are relatively restrained in their behavior. They remain fully clothed throughout the scene after each removes an outer garment, and Helen appears more dreamy than aroused. Whereas some other productions show the couple ducking beneath the covers at the end and imply a frantic climax, in the Zurich version they remain fully visible in the final embrace.

One particularly effective scene in the Zurich production is Act I, Scene VI, when Orestes enters with two Corinthian hetairas to sing the couplets "Au cabaret du Labyrinthe" and the three interact with Calchas. Orestes is played sassily by the young Romanian mezzo Liliana Nikiteanu. The two hetairas Parthenis and Laeana, played by Lisa Larsson and Ulrika Precht, wear skimpy clothing and extravagantly colorful curly wigs. As indicated by the refrain vocables "Tsing la la" that swoop down by a ninth, this scene is designed to be ridiculous – in a charming coincidence, the woman who created the role of Orestes was named Léa Silly – and this cast accentuates its charm and silliness. At the same time, Orestes' commentary – his cynicism about his aunt's constant appeal to Fate and his confidence that his papa will pay for his entertainment with tax money – brings out the social critique that is central to the genre. The young women flirt shamelessly with Calchas, pointing out that they too have been affected by Fate – how else did one of them get the opportunity to join the ballet? – and the priest charmingly confesses in a final monologue that he is strongly tempted to partake in their hedonistic lifestyle.

Théâtre du Châtelet 2000

This Parisian production was the first of two Offenbach productions at the Théâtre du Châtelet to employ the creative team of stage director Laurent Pelly, conductor Marc Minkowski, set designer Chantal Thomas, choreographer Laura Scozzi, and singers Felicity Lott and Yann Beuron as the female and male leads. It was followed by *La Grande Duchesse de Gérolstein* in 2004 (also available on DVD). This series of Offenbach productions had begun in 1997 at the Opéra de Lyon with *Orphée aux enfers*, featuring most of the same directing team, with Yann Beuron as Orpheus and Natalie Dessay as Eurydice.

Though from a later generation than Harnoncourt, Minkowski has followed a similar path in his approach to repertoire. He began with a focus on Baroque music, founding the group Les Musiciens du Louvre at the early age of nineteen. With this group, "he explored and expanded French repertoire and Handel before delving into Mozart, Rossini, Offenbach, and Wagner" (Minkowski, 2025). He has also collaborated with opera companies and orchestras throughout Europe and the United States. His conducting style is animated and energetic, bringing a wide range of music to life.

The two later productions take full advantage of the special vocal and acting talent of Dame Lott, who began her operatic career in the 1970s and is also a notable performer of classical song. She began to add operetta roles to her repertoire in the 1980s with *The Merry Widow*, and this lighter genre became a more significant emphasis for her in the 1990s (Lott, 2024). For me, she is clearly the center of both Châtelet productions, in which she frolics and takes great delight in the humorous and erotic elements of operetta. The staging team makes no effort to conceal her age, so it is evident that she was in her fifties at this time – older than we would presume Helen or the Grand Duchess to be. The *Grande Duchesse* production in particular makes her age into part of the humor of the story, whose title character – supposedly a young woman about to be betrothed – becomes so enamored of a handsome soldier that she puts him in command of her army just as a war breaks out, contrary to the advice of her cabinet and military officers.

This *Belle Hélène* is presented as a kind of play within a play. During the overture, we see a suburban bedroom from about the 1950s, with a husband already asleep while his bored wife takes her sleeping pills. The bed remains onstage throughout all three acts and even serves as the boat on which Helen and Paris fly away at the end. This framing explains the operetta as the fantasies of a frustrated woman who imagines herself as the mythical Helen. Quite different from Vesselina Kasarova's languid representation of the character, Felicity

Lott's housewife-as-Helen revels in her ability to excite men and express her erotic nature.

Supporting the transplant of the story into modern times, the mythological scenes are staged to show Greece as a kind of historical theme park. In Act I, when the kings make their opening entrances and grandly announce themselves, the chorus is dressed as a tour group, led by a guide who presents this ceremony as a historical quiz, testing their knowledge of the *Iliad*. During the opening music for Act II, the omnipresent bed is seen in the middle of an archaeological dig whose workers engage in a choreographed dance with their shovels, brooms, and wheelbarrows. This awareness of the story as ancient history adds a new layer to the anachronisms already built into the operetta.

In Act I, Paris introduces himself as a shepherd; when Helen asks him where his sheep are, he vaguely replies "over there on the mountain" (Tout là-bas, là-bas, là-bas dans la montagne). Mythology tells us that because of a prophetic dream, Paris was not raised in Priam's court, but was abandoned, left for dead, and then raised by shepherds. His identity as a shepherd adds a comical element to this production's version of the love duet. Helen is resting on her bed, awaiting the dream of Paris that Calchas has agreed to send her. She is fully covered up in a white dress with a scarf tucked around her neck (which she later removes when Paris asks to see her shoulders). Paris enters disguised as a slave and sings about her beauty as she sleeps. She then awakes, perceives that he is there and leaps to the conclusion that this is her dream (Paris quickly removing his shirt as she sings); he goes along with this as they begin the duet, whose refrain is on the lines "Yes, it is a dream ... it is only a sweet dream of love" (Oui, c'est un rêve, ce n'est qu'un rêve, un doux rêve d'amour).

Just after they begin to sing, who should enter the stage but a group of sheep (represented by dancers wearing fleeces and sheep's heads) – evidently, Paris's flock has come down from the mountain. Along with beautiful singing and Lott's comic delight in an illicit romance, the sheep truly make this scene. At first, they quietly graze; when the couple begin to discuss the comparison of Helen and Venus, they raptly listen, sometimes rocking along with particularly sinuous phrases, sometimes leaning their heads on their comically visible hands. Finally, when Helen agrees to kiss Paris as Venus did, the sheep divide into pairs, affectionately nuzzling. At the end of the duet, Paris and Helen are swaying blissfully behind a sheet. They dive down onto the mattress just as Menelaus returns with his luggage, by which time the sheep have mysteriously vanished.

Hamburg 2014

This production used a long-standing team known as Barbe & Doucet: stage director and choreographer Renaud Doucet and set and costume designer André Barbe, who have worked together on numerous productions, beginning in 2000. As they point out in their self-description, they bring together the worlds of North America and Europe, as Barbe is French-Canadian and Doucet French. They represent their goals in the following statement, which defines their distinction from post-modern performance style:

> By way of this unusual combination Barbe & Doucet made their mark, with their theory of two worlds: a return to the origins in order to recreate within the present a work which manages to capture what was pertinent in the first place. The researching of emotions together with the pure pleasure evoked by performance are key elements of what Barbe & Doucet pursue, elements which are often discarded in post-modern mise-en-scene by way of serving a radical deconstruction in a quixotic quest for universality.
>
> Barbe & Doucet have defined their own way of deconstructing as a point of departure but it is in their particular way of re-appropriating and reconstructing that allows them to offer the public a work which, by way of a curious familiarity, opens the doors of perception while at the same time granting access to intelligent emotions by way of re-temporalising the work, by reinvigorating its pertinence. (Barbe & Doucet, 2017)

To paraphrase, this directing team moves original works to more modern settings to avoid letting them be museum pieces. By making some changes, these directors attempt to bring to life what the work was about in the first place. Their version of *La belle Hélène* does so through choices very similar to those made fourteen years earlier in the Paris production. Like that one, it is set in the mid twentieth century, in this case on a 1960s cruise ship. The other notable similarity is that they also construct a back story during the overture when the woman we will soon see in the role of Helen approaches the ship with her unexciting husband. He purchases some statues of antiquities on the dock, and then a very large statue being lifted by a crane hits his wife on the head, so that she has to be carried onto the ship on a stretcher. Her episode of unconsciousness apparently leads her to cast herself in the role of Helen. Just as in the Châtelet production, the story is presented as the fantasy of a frustrated housewife. The costumes of most characters remain those of sailors and holiday travelers. The uniformed captain of the ship takes the role of Calchas.

The purchase of statues also sets up a homoerotic element, showing that Menelaus is more drawn to men than women, which helps to explain his wife's readiness to explore a new sexual liaison. While she appears relatively frumpy at the beginning in a pink coat and straw hat, her beauty and sensuality become more evident later in the show – this is a different strategy from the Paris production, in which Helen's appearance does not change.

The Hamburg production is notable for its extensive use of visual references to popular culture of the 1960s. Not only are the clothing and hairstyles based on the styles of that time, but also there are many specific references to celebrities, brand names, and typical pastimes of the 1960s. Here are a few examples:

- Orestes' clothes, hairstyle, and glasses make him a close double of the character Austin Powers (played by Mike Myers) in films satirizing 1960s spy movies.
- In Act III, when Paris enters disguised as the "high" priest of Venus, he looks like Jimi Hendrix, and as he sings about how Venus wants everyone to be happy, he distributes marijuana joints to the crowd. Helen then enters wearing a scarf and large glasses that make her look like Jackie Onassis.[6]
- Helen's attendant Bacchis looks and behaves like a sulky teenager of the time period, chewing gum and frequently rolling her eyes in annoyance.
- Among the Greek kings, Achilles plays electric guitar, while the two Ajaxes wear sports uniforms, referencing both the Dutch soccer team Ajax and the brand-name cleanser (first produced in 1947 with a new type of cleanser released in 1962), whose logo is sewn onto their shirts.
- When Agamemnon makes an entrance, the chorus shouts "Aga" – perhaps referring to the Aga Khan IV, who had inherited this title in 1957 and was a prominent member of the jet set.
- Similarly, the logo of the Apple company is used in reference to Paris giving the apple to Venus – another reference to brand names, anachronistic even in relation to the time frame of the production, since the company was founded in 1976.

Jennifer Larmore plays Helen. Like Lott, she was in her mid-fifties at the time of the show, but the production de-emphasizes her age. In the love duet, for example, she wears a low-cut rosy-orange dress that shows off her breasts. She is elaborately made up with false eyelashes and red lipstick, whereas Lott is skinny, dressed modestly in white, and wears minimal makeup. During this scene, Hamburg's Paris, played by Korean tenor Jun-Sang Han (a member of the Hamburg Staatsoper company at that time), looks notably silly in a sailor suit, curly blond wig, and horn-rimmed glasses. These two performers display

---

[6] On their first album, *Fig. 14* (1980), the Boston-based New Wave band Human Sexual Response wrote "Jackie Onassis," with the opening lines "I want to be Jackie Onassis, I want to wear a pair of dark sunglasses." These lines were borrowed in 1996 in the song "Tire Me" by Rage Against the Machine. See Sullivan (2017).

more ravenous and overt sexuality than in the two productions described earlier – Helen brings out a whip and handcuffs, they mimic the moves of intercourse under a faux fur blanket, and she begins smoking a cigarette just before Menelaus appears.

At the end of the operetta (Act III, Scenes VII–VIII), Paris returns, disguised as the augur of Venus. This takes place on a deck of the cruise ship that features a swimming pool filled with hollow blue balls that mimic watery motion when people move through and pretend to swim. The company is dressed in swimming costumes – some modest and others topless – and several men wear Hawaiian-style flower-print outfits. As the chorus begins to sing penitently to welcome the supposed priest, Paris moves through the crowd with his large Afro hairdo and sunglasses, giving the two-fingered peace symbol with both hands. While singing the Tyrolienne, admonishing them to be joyful, he pulls exaggeratedly huge marijuana joints out of the cloth bag hanging on his shoulder and tosses them to the crowd. Paris approaches Calchas, who is looking glum about his rival, and offers him a joint as well, pulling out a lighter to assist. The company dances joyfully, smoking their joints and waving their arms, and some holding tambourines.

After Paris explains that he must take the queen to Cythera, Helen enters wearing light but enveloping summer clothing, a scarf around her head, and huge sunglasses. Evidently depressed, she is eating from a large container of ice cream and then attempts but fails to light a cigarette. She becomes angry on being asked to go on this journey, but after Paris quietly reveals his identity, she unwraps her head and agrees, by singing a joyful, fiercely ornamented version of her usual line "C'est la fatalité," complete with all sorts of trills, improvised melodic gestures, and imitations of the hand gestures singers use in practice to get proper vocal placement. (This phrase lasts a full minute and a quarter.) Menelaus, glad that his wife has conceded, joins the hands of the two lovers amid general rejoicing, and they climb into a little two-seater flying machine. As they float upward, Paris removes his wig and sunglasses, announcing tauntingly to Menelaus that he is truly Paris, taking away his wife. Helen waves happily as if they are on a parade float, as the chorus dances joyfully and Agamemnon reacts first with confusion and then despair.

Berlin 2014

Barrie Kosky, stage director for this production, was the artistic director at the Komische Oper from 2012–13 through 2021–22. Kosky has described himself as a "gay, Jewish kangaroo," referring to his Australian origin and linking himself with groups often viewed as minorities and outsiders. During his tenure at the Komische Oper, he made a point of paying homage to Berlin's Jewish heritage and its assertive LGBTQ community. While he directs both operas and operettas, the operetta genre, already built on social criticism, particularly connects with his penchant for satire, camp, and gay eroticism. Interestingly, his *Hélène* eschewed the more direct political references found in some other productions of the work, as though the very act of flaunting sexual difference became the only political statement needed.

As previously discussed, the Châtelet and Hamburg productions are set in particular decades and make many references to those time periods, while the Zurich production is time-neutral, mixing and matching styles in costumes and sets. In that respect, the Berlin production is more similar to Zurich. The costumes suggest various times in the twentieth century – for example, Helen sometimes wears a skimpy sequin dress, and Act III features 1920s bathing costumes – with a distinct tendency to titillate the audience; the most iconic example is the male chorus on roller skates wearing overall shorts with holes cut in the back to display their bare buttocks. Calchas's "thunder" machine is a gramophone with a huge bell, suggesting the late nineteenth or early twentieth century. This device plays many musical quotations ranging from Beethoven to Mahler – that is, some preceding Offenbach's time and others from later. Two French songs from the early twentieth century are also quoted by being sung. Offenbach's music is supplemented and sometimes supplanted by musical references. Some of the pieces quoted include

- The Jewish folk song "Hava Nagila" – briefly in Act I, then used often to cheer on competitors during the riddle contest;
- The opening of Beethoven's Fifth Symphony – at moments referencing Fate;
- A dramatic motive from Verdi's *La Forza del Destino* – at especially dramatic moments;
- Siegfried's funeral march from Wagner's *Götterdämmerung* – after Beethoven's Fifth at the first mention of "la fatalité";
- The overture of Wagner's *Tannhäuser*, Pilgrim's Chorus theme – played by Calchas to soothe himself;
- The opening of Mahler's Sixth Symphony – as dance music for Venus's messenger dove;
- The "Mirror aria" from Gounod's *Faust* – sung by Helen just before she meets Paris;
- Brünnhilde's music as she mourns Siegfried in *Götterdämmerung* – just after Helen meets Paris;
- The Harry Warren song "Chattanooga Choo Choo" – after Paris decodes the riddle and the answer is "locomotive";

- LPs that Helen plays when trying to go to sleep: Elsa's aria "Einsam in trüben Tagen" from *Lohengrin*, "Träume" from Wagner's Wesendonck Lieder, both rejected; then she accepts a jazz song, "You are the one for me";
- The French song "Non, je ne regrette rien" (No, I regret nothing), composed by Michel DuMont and strongly associated with performer Edith Piaf – sung by Helen between Acts II and III;
- Jacques Brel, "Ne me quitte pas" (Do not leave me) – sung by Menelaus during Act III.

Throughout the performance, this production adds comic elements that tend toward the slapstick; a few examples are as follows.

- Calchas (Stefan Sevenich) is played in a fat suit, with a protruding belly. His size becomes a joke in itself: he faints and others push on his belly in an attempt to revive him; he roller-skates and falls down; and he shows his ability to pirouette gracefully despite his awkwardness.
- In Helen's first scene with Calchas, they play the roles of human and dog: he approaches her in a doglike way, she caresses his belly, and so on.
- At various moments, Helen exclaims (in English) "Don't speak!" This happens first when it is in the libretto (in French or German) and then becomes a kind of shtick for her character. Her other shtick is to make baaing sounds when she is with Paris, referring to his profession as a shepherd. Such behaviors are often inserted right in the middle of her lines. The result is an arbitrary mix of styles that resembles works written for twentieth-century performance artists, such as Luciano Berio's *Sequenza III* and Cathy Berberian's *Stripsody*. This production does not aim for consistency of characters or a steady flow of action but delights instead in interruption and discontinuity.
- Menelaus (Peter Renz) wears an eyepatch and moves about in a wheelchair until he suddenly begins to walk while arguing with Helen during Act II. After that, he remains mobile for the rest of the show.
- There are interesting choices involving crossdressing. Helen's maid Bacchis is played by a man with beard and mustache (Hakan T. Aslan), yet he moves in a mincing walk that is exaggeratedly female. Orestes, as usual, is played by a woman, Karolina Gumos. Partway through the "Tsing-la-la" aria, Gumos strips off her male clothing to reveal short tight female clothing and then continues to play as a woman in this scene, but her costume in Act III is more androgynous. The silent role of the dove sent as a messenger from Venus dances in caricatured ballet style, often en pointe, but is played by a man, Karlheinz Oettel.

These features and other similar performance choices lead to a strange experience. For a spectator familiar with the work, this production is like watching the original operetta with interruptions and an overlay of slapstick comedy. For audience members who do not know the work, it may not be clear what is original and what has been added; the overall effect is a mix of operetta, sitcom, and stand-up comedy.

American soprano Nicole Chevalier, who played Helen, was in her thirties. Her costumes and make up emphasized her thin, angular body, and neither blocking nor choreography was designed to make her appear traditionally beautiful. This is interesting in contrast to the other productions discussed earlier: those in Zurich and Hamburg made a point of emphasizing Helen's voluptuousness, while the Paris production also featured a skinny performer, but showed her (Felicity Lott) as very excited about sensual experiences. Chevalier's Helen, by contrast, is capricious and seems disconnected from her own sensuality. This brings us to the consideration of how the Berlin production represents the adultery scene.

One surprising omission in this production is that Helen does not ask Calchas to send her a dream of Paris. That request is important to the plot, since it shows why she believes (or says she does) that their encounter is a dream, so it is not clear why this dialogue was cut. In the Berlin production, Helen uses the gramophone and samples a few musical selections, rejecting two Wagner excerpts and wildly tossing the records across the stage, until she is finally lulled to sleep by the jazz song "You are the one for me." The furniture on stage is not a bed, but a very long sofa. While she sleeps, Paris enters in dinner jacket and white tie, pushes aside the gramophone and cues the orchestra so that he can sing about her beauty; she then begins to sing the duet with him. At first, she keeps her distance; when he touches her breasts, she pushes him over the back of the sofa. However, after asking him to compare her beauty with that of Venus, she does a mock swimming motion toward him on the sofa and blatantly puts her mouth over his genitals (though he remains clothed). He unzips her dress and they enter into closer contact in a deliberately awkward way. They simulate sexual moves, with her on top swinging an imaginary lasso. This presentation of the scene is perhaps the most stylized among the four productions.

I find the opening of Act III to be one of the most successful sections of this production. The act opens with a chorus followed by Orestes' song, describing the strange sexual frenzy that Venus has inflicted on Greece. As they sing, chorus members spin parasols that create rotating spiral patterns while dancing energetically in their 1920s beachwear. Following this number, the Greek kings enter, sit down on the long couch, and discuss what to do about the problematic sexual license as they diligently apply sunscreen, helping one another to access places that are difficult to reach. Helen and Menelaus begin the argument about her "dream," during which Menelaus suddenly stands and leaves his wheelchair, to which she delightedly exclaims "Schatzi, du laufst!" (Honey, you're walking!). Next come the couplets in which Helen threatens her husband: if he is complaining so much about a dream, just wait until it becomes reality! Her quirky petulant style works well in this number, during which she eventually stomps on Agamemnon's foot. This whole sequence, leading into the grand trio that parodies *Guillaume Tell*, is particularly effective because it displays the production's whimsical approach to staging without adding too many insertions that can disrupt the flow of the drama.

Overall, the production's use of pastiche, along with frequent references and reversals of gender stereotypes, puts it in the category of post-modernism. It could be argued that by presenting the work in this way, Kosky is simply magnifying what is already there.[7] The original show emphasizes deliberate incongruity as it moves from staged rituals to silly parlor games to parody of grand opera. Serious and poignant moments are intermingled with idiotic ones. Kosky compounds these nonsensical juxtapositions by adding more crazy elements – wheelchair, fat suit, roller skates, tag lines, and musical quotations – treating Offenbach much as Offenbach treated the Greek myth. The intended effect may be to give present-day audiences a jolting and incongruous experience similar to that of 1860s audiences – yet these additions and interruptions also obscure the (dis)continuities of the original work. By treating this operetta as an exemplar of an old tradition that needs to be updated, the Berlin version disguises the radical and post-modern nature of the original.[8]

Comparative Reflections

These four productions display a wide range of creative expression, using various tools that add layers of meaning to the original show. All use stage sets and particularly costumes as a strong interpretive element. The Paris and Hamburg productions frame the plot with stories of frustrated twentieth-century women. The Berlin production utilizes numerous external musical references, creating intertextuality as the outside music comments on characters and events.

---

[7] While post-modernism is often described as a phenomenon of the later twentieth century, some of its characteristics can be found in earlier works. In a course he taught at the University of Chicago in the 1990s, Charles Rosen, while discussing Ludwig Tieck's highly self-conscious 1797 play *Der gestiefelte Kater* (Puss in Boots) declared that "post-modernism was born approximately one day after modernism."

[8] Rebecca Schmid expresses a similar thought: "As Kosky rightly points out, the opera is rife with a mix of eroticism and nonsense that verges on the surreal. The mythic theme also lends itself easily to an updated take. But there is no need to dismember Offenbach's energetic, masterfully constructed and witty score in order to achieve that goal." (Schmid, 2014.)

All the productions encounter the question of how to represent Helen, supposedly the most beautiful woman in the world. Should this be taken literally or made part of the satire? Their choices of performer and performing style are quite varied. There were two older and two younger performers in this role, and two who were skinny, and two more voluptuous. The women's attitudes toward sex and eroticism varied from Lott's childlike delight to Chevalier's cynical alienation.

There were also different approaches to the political and social critique that characterized the original show. The symbolic visual and verbal references on the Zurich costumes made this version perhaps the most abstract and timeless, though it did emphasize the libretto's references to taxation that benefits the rich at the expense of ordinary people. (One further example from that production is discussed in Section 4.) The Hamburg and Paris productions satirized the times and settings that they created: 1960s pop culture and the commodification of ancient Greece, respectively. The Berlin production shunned specific political references, substituting a joyfully campy challenge to norms of gender and respectability. All in all, the variety found in these four versions affirms the presence of Regietheater and the wide range of interpretations that characterizes operetta performance in recent decades.

3 Revivals of Kálmán's *Die Herzogin von Chicago* in 2004 and 2016

Kálmán's *Die Herzogin von Chicago* is diametrically opposed to Offenbach's *La belle Hélène* in three ways. Chronologically, with its premiere in April 1928, it came late in this relatively short-lived genre whose heyday lasted about eighty years. Geographically, it represents Austria-Hungary rather than France. In spirit, it might be argued to be self-consciously nostalgic, an autumnal tribute to operetta and the now-lost Dual Empire, as opposed to the bold sassy attitude toward both modern French life and classical myth that characterizes the Offenbach – but it also played with new sounds and ideas, particularly the early American jazz that had captivated Europe since World War I. Baranello describes *Die Herzogin* as "a work that looks both forward and backward, an example of the negotiations between operetta's traditions and new realities" (Baranello, 2021, p. 160).

One circumstance this operetta shares with *La belle Hélène*, however, is that it was frequently revived from the late twentieth into the early twenty-first century. Unlike Offenbach's work, *Die Herzogin von Chicago* had sunk into obscurity, propelled largely by its classification as "decadent music" (*entartete Musik*) by the Nazis. A 1998 Decca recording of the full work conducted by

Richard Bonynge brought the operetta more attention, and several companies presented it in the following years. The fiftieth anniversary of the composer's death in 2003 was an incentive for many companies to feature his operettas, and the composer's daughter Yvonne Kálmán favored this one. She was also very open to revisions and alterations, which likely drew directors to the piece. In this section, I compare and contrast the 2004 Vienna Volksoper production – the first in Vienna since 1928 – with the 2016 Budapest Operetta Theatre production, incorporating information from interviews I conducted with leading figures in both productions. The Vienna interviews took place in 2009, and I have discussed them at greater length elsewhere (Feurzeig, 2016). The Budapest interviews took place in 2017. These two productions reflect extremely different ideas about how to approach 1920s operetta. It is noteworthy that the Budapest team was not aware of the Vienna production twelve years earlier, although it was available on DVD; they had encountered the work through a concert performance by the Komische Oper in Berlin (Lőrinczy, 2017).

Die Herzogin von Chicago – Background

This work has some interesting background in real life. The main female character, Miss Mary Lloyd, is very similar to Chicago heiress Ginevra King Pirie (1898–1980). Like Mary, Ginevra King was an arrogant young woman strongly associated with a group of similar young ladies, and she hailed from the northern Chicago suburb of Lake Forest, Illinois.

> Collectively known as the Big Four (a name they bestowed on themselves), they were *the* socialites of their era. The exclusive group didn't allow new members, and each wore a rose-gold pinkie ring with *The Big Four 1914* engraved on the inner band. They rarely went out in public without each other, were either loved or reviled by everyone who knew about them, and, with the brashness of the young and rich, didn't care about what anybody thought. (Diamond, 2012.)

In her late teens, Ginevra King was passionately involved with F. Scott Fitzgerald, then a student at Princeton, for about two years, and she was his model for the character Daisy Buchanan in *The Great Gatsby*. As in the novel, she married a much wealthier man rather than Fitzgerald. Following her second marriage to the owner of a major Chicago department store, she remained part of Chicago's elite society for her whole life. Her fellow "Big Four" friend Edith Cummings, who became a famous golfer, was probably the model for Jordan Baker in *The Great Gatsby*. These arrogant young women, accustomed to being admired and feted for their beauty and wealth, resemble Miss Mary Lloyd and her friends. Even the notion that they represented a kind of American aristocracy is found in a quote from a biography of Fitzgerald's wife Zelda: "[h]e met and fell in love with Ginevra King, a rich and wildly popular visitor from Chicago, who at sixteen had the social ease of a young duchess" (Milford, 1970, p. 28).

This group of young women resembles the "Ladies' Eccentric Club" of the operetta. While it is hard to ascertain whether anyone in Europe would have heard of them, Ginevra King was sufficiently prominent in the United States to be featured on the cover of *Town and Country* magazine in July 1918, and *The Great Gatsby* was published in 1925, three years before the operetta.

Moving in another direction, the name "Mary Lloyd" has two possible connections. One is an English music hall singer whose stage name was Marie Lloyd (1870–1922). The other is a Welsh wassailing tradition called "Mari Lwyd," in which revelers carry a horse's skull from house to house, requesting to be let in. After "an improvised battle of rhyme and verse" they enter the home, where "they are given cakes and ales, the Mari Lwyd causes some mischief and everyone moves on to the next house" (Brett, 2022). Another description states that "[t]he Mari Lwyd would try and gain entry to houses via song. The merrymen would explain why they needed to enter and the occupant of the house would sing why they can't be let in. This would go back and forth until the occupant didn't have any more reasons to not let them in" (Rhinwedd, 2024).

As with the Big Four, it is unclear how and whether the librettists would have had any knowledge of these similar names and their associations, one with the musical theater stage and the other with the idea of an ongoing debate (such as the jazz-csárdás conflict) that leads to one person creating mischief in someone else's home (such as Mary Lloyd's renovations of the Sylvarian palace).

Die Herzogin von Chicago – Plot

This synopsis is based on the *Regiebuch*. It should be noted that the show was very long on the first night and remained so even after having been cut. As Kevin Clarke explains, "On the basis of the premiere, the reaction of the public in the weeks after the premiere, and the reviews, Kálmán, Brammer and Grünwald begin reworking and cutting the piece the day after the premiere. For, according to Marischka, *Die Herzogin* is one hour and twenty minutes too long" (Clarke, 2007, p. 201). Both the productions we will discuss had to shorten it considerably.

The Vorspiel (Prologue) takes place in a Budapest bar-restaurant called the Grille américaine, whose manager and Gypsy bandleader are discussing an ongoing shift in social prestige. Instead of royal and aristocratic patrons, the bar now prefers business owners, particularly those with American connections. American jazz dances such as the foxtrot and Charleston have also come into fashion.

Sandor Boris, Crown Prince of Sylvaria, enters the venue, but whimsically exchanges places with one of his attendants. The bandleader instantly recognizes Sandor Boris, an old acquaintance, who is outraged to see this wonderful fiddler expected to play the saxophone. The band plays a "Beethoven foxtrot" – a new arrangement of the opening of the Fifth Symphony – and the prince breaks in, demanding waltz and csárdás instead; he is also horrified to see one of the Hungarian musicians wearing blackface.

The American heiress Miss Mary Lloyd now enters, accompanied by her attendant, the Jewish-American Johnny James Bondy, whose family roots are in Sylvaria. Her father, a Chicago billionaire, has just purchased oil rights in Sylvaria. Mary has come to Europe to participate in a contest among members of the "Ladies' Eccentric Club" in New York; the winner will be the lady who purchases whatever in Europe is most difficult to buy. Learning that the Crown Prince is there, she whimsically demands to dance a Charleston with him. Bondy approaches the royal party and presents this request to the actual Prince (posing as his attendant), who refuses, but informs the Americans that the Prince would gladly dance a waltz or Hungarian csárdás with Miss Lloyd.

The exciting finale that follows alternates between Mary's musical sections featuring jazz and the Prince's sections featuring European sentimental and dance music. She glorifies the American dollar, while he expresses his appreciation for the old ways and the privileges of his upper-class heritage. The Prince embraces the Gypsy primás, demonstrating their shared musical taste. This relationship recalls stories of historical figures such as King Ludwig II of Bavaria and Crown Prince Rudolf of Austria, whose closest confidants were their coachmen and valets rather than their aristocratic companions.

Ultimately, the csárdás triumphs to conclude the prologue, which has set up the broad conflict of this work. The brash American sphere of money, business, and opportunity are pitted against the traditional European emphasis on hierarchy and tradition. Each culture has its symbolic musical style: American jazz dances, modern but also linked to "primitive" African traditions, are contrasted with the European sentiment and sophistication expressed in Wienerlieder, waltz, and fiery csárdás. The sizzling anger between Miss Lloyd and Prince Sandor Boris as they defend their musical cultures clearly has the potential for transformation into sexual attraction.

Act I takes place in the ancestral castle of Sylvaria, opening with a ceremonial song in honor of the prince's birthday. His chief ministers tell him that Mary Lloyd is in town with her entourage of a full jazz band and dancing girls. The

Prince welcomes a chorus of young princes from the kingdom of Morenia, all in military uniform, who bring birthday greetings and a present of a doll representing Sandor Boris. They sing a charming march about a military parade.

Bondy arrives, requests an audience, and announces that Mary wants to buy the castle. He and the ministers quickly negotiate, agreeing to a price of six million dollars. Mary enters and immediately starts planning her renovations, including making the throne room into a dance floor. Next, Princess Rosemarie of Morenia arrives; she has a lisp, and the ministers advise her to avoid words including the letter "S" when she meets the Prince, as they are hoping for a betrothal. He enters and is charmed by the princess along with her lisp – but the two agree that neither one of them wants to marry another prince or princess. They sing a duet about the imagined pleasures of ordinary people.

The Prince and Mary have a tête-à-tête in which she tells him how sorry she is for princes; in the duet "Armer Prinz," she explains that she once had a doll just like the plaything brought by the Morenian children, but when she cut it open, she realized that it was stuffed with ordinary straw. Still deceived by his previous playful role exchange, she does not know that she is speaking with the Prince himself. Rosemarie and Bondy are also drawn together, especially as they realize that each has a disability: her lisp and his Jewish heritage. (He calls himself an "Israelittle.") They also discover that each is supposed to marry for the sake of "the firm." All these interactions signal that the two couples planned by their families will soon be switching partners.

When the Prince reappears and is greeted by fanfares, Mary realizes who he is and apologizes for what she said when she believed him to be someone else. He makes a formal announcement that he has decided to sell the castle, devoting the full purchase price to the needs of his people. Mary is touched by his decision, as he told her earlier about all the history and memories he associates with this building. To conclude Act I, she privately instructs Bondy to send a telegram to her father, announcing that she has purchased the castle and will now work on acquiring the Prince as well.

Act II is set in the same castle, newly renovated by Mary, who is hosting a party to show off the new decor. The chief ministers are delighted with the country's improved finances, and Bondy informs Mary that they have taken over several Sylvarian industries. Mary's American girlfriends arrive and admire the palace, as does the Prince, though he regrets some of the changes. The two admit that each has secretly been taking lessons in the other's dance: Mary's jazz director is teaching Sandor Boris the Charleston, while his Gypsy primás is teaching her to waltz. They agree that the Charleston is the American form of the Csárdás.

The Prince's chief ministers secretly plan a marriage between Sandor and Mary, planning to declare her the Duchess of Chicago to overcome her lack of a pedigree. They also offer an order of nobility to Bondy, who requests a Star of David rather than the Cross of St. Michael. Benjamin Lloyd, Mary's father, unexpectedly arrives from Chicago. She tells him about her plan to marry the Prince, but when she describes the contest, he doubts her love for the Prince and advises against the marriage.

His new aristocratic title emboldens Bondy to offer Princess Rosemarie his hand in marriage. She accepts, and they sing a joyful duet about how they will listen to jazz together in the penthouse of his Chicago skyscraper. The refrain "Im Himmel spielt auch schon die Jazzband" (In Heaven, the jazz band is already playing) likens life at the top of a skyscraper to the next world.

Mary tells her father that though she began to woo him because of the competition, she now truly loves Sandor. Mr. Lloyd meets the Prince, interrogates him about his profession, and gives his blessing to the match. Mary persuades the Prince that Americans are susceptible to romance, and they sing the charming duet "Rose der Prairie" in which they play the roles of a cowboy and an Indian girl in love. Sandor meets the American girls, who declare that Mary has won the contest and explain it to Sandor Boris, who is deeply offended. His ministers reluctantly show him the telegram Mary sent to her father at the end of the previous act. After a grand ceremony to declare Mary the Duchess of Chicago, the plan is to announce her engagement to the Prince, but instead he declares his intent to marry Rosemarie. Just as in Kálmán's *Gräfin Mariza*, Act II ends with the discovery of a written document that leads to misunderstanding, a break-up, and general unhappiness.

In the Nachspiel (Postlude), the two chief ministers of Sylvaria meet the actual King of Sylvaria, Sandor Boris's uncle, in the Grille américaine. King Pankraz XXVII is a ridiculous old man who lives a life of pleasure outside Sylvaria. In operetta terms, he is a third-act comedian – the most famous role in this category is that of Frosch, the jailer in *Die Fledermaus* – and as such, his scene includes deliberate references to other operettas. He enters accompanied by two young women, Joujou and Loulou, their names taken from Lehár's *Merry Widow*. Being hard of hearing, he claims that the two young ladies speak only French, though they converse in Berlin dialect. Pankraz is extremely disappointed that the plan for Sandor Boris to marry Mary Lloyd has failed, since her wealth is necessary for the insolvent kingdom. He comes up with an alternate plan: as the judge says in *Trial by Jury*, "I will marry her myself!" The King then quotes *Die Fledermaus* by singing the refrain of Orlofsky's aria, "Chacun à son gout!" The ministers are delighted with his new plan to retain

Miss Lloyd for the Sylvarian royal family, a scheme similar to a plot twist near the end of *The Merry Widow*.

Prince Sandor Boris appears with his entourage and learns that Mary has been in the bar every night with a mysterious young man, listening to Wienerlieder and csárdás. In view of his engagement with Rosemarie, he attempts to suppress his strong jealousy and requests some music, but when the band begins with the music he preferred in the prologue, he asks for something more modern. He also reassures the musician in blackface that he is no longer angry. He and his officers begin to sing "Rose der Prairie," and the Prince seizes the saxophone to play the refrain. Clearly, the reversal of musical preferences symbolizes an imminent romantic reconciliation.

Mary enters flirting with the mysterious stranger and receives a marriage proposal from King Pankraz, much to her dismay. She and the king sing a duet, mostly in disconnected French phrases to indicate how little French they know (another reference to *Fledermaus*). A newsboy enters with an "extra" edition, bringing the news to Sandor Boris that Rosemarie has run away with Bondy and they have gotten married at the American Embassy. The stranger provokes a confrontation with Sandor, but instead of a duel, it produces an explanation: this man represents the Fox-Paramount film studio, and he is in Europe in pursuit of a real-life story to film. The whole set of events that have occurred so far makes for a perfect film, but as the American public requires a "happy end," it is necessary for Mary and Sandor to reunite. They do so joyfully, and the curtain falls as all dance a "slowfox mit Mary."

Two Productions

Table 2 lists the two productions discussed here and their directing teams.

My commentary will combine what I learned from interviews with observations from watching the DVD of the Vienna production and both a live performance and an online video of the one in Budapest.

Vienna 2004

The Vienna script was adapted by stage director Dominik Wilgenbus with operetta scholar Stefan Frey, whose biography of Kálmán had appeared the year before. Both are extremely familiar with the operetta genre and its history, and they were well aware of this work's liminal nature as an early example of the revue style and jazz-operetta fusion that would both continue into the 1930s. They approached the piece with a healthy respect for its historical place. As Wilgenbus explained, their two main goals for the

Table 2 Productions of *Die Herzogin von Chicago*

Company	Year	Adaptation, dialogue	Conductor	Stage director	Sets/Costumes
Vienna Volksoper	2004	Stefan Frey, Dominik Wilgenbus	Tamás Bolba	Dominik Wilgenbus	Balázs Horesnyi / Rita Velich
Budapest Operetta Theatre	2016	Attila Lőrinczy	Lászlo Makláry	Attila Béres	Alexander Weig / Gerlinde Höglhammer and Christine Sadjina-Höfer

adaptation were to shorten the original and make it flow more effectively (Wilgenbus, 2009). In place of the original structure of Vorspiel – Act I – Act II – Nachspiel, they designed a two-act structure. Seeing the confrontation in the Grille américaine as the work's strongest scene, they moved it to the middle of Act I rather than have the work start with the best part (Frey, 2009). They also shuffled some of the action so that after a new opening scene in New York, the scenes move back and forth between the Budapest club and Sylvaria.

The newly written scene begins at the Eccentric Ladies' Club in New York, where the members are watching the end of a film. They tease the unresponsive Mary for being without feeling; she states that American girls use money to get what they want and places a bet with them that she can purchase herself a Prince in Europe. This scene was added "so that we don't just narrate this, but show it" (Wilgenbus, 2009). Bondy is also introduced, as the film projectionist; he tells Mary about the Prince of Sylvaria, and she imperiously hires him as her secretary. The remainder of the scene shows their sea voyage to Europe.

To counterbalance the Prince's rude and violent behavior in the Grille américaine scene, this production brings out his charm. For example, his interaction with Rosemarie's younger siblings shows his affection for children, and his duet with Rosemarie, through alterations in the text, emphasizes even more than the original the rueful feelings both have about their arranged marriage. (One clever addition: the refrain ends with "O Rosemarie!" In the altered version, that is replaced the second time by "O Monarchie!")

One important alteration was the transformation of part of "Rose der Prairie" into an animated cartoon sequence. After opening the scene as live actors, the singers are transformed first into animated versions of themselves, which then are transmuted into the imaginary cowboy and Indian girl. A comical love scene between the two cartoon characters is projected, complete with cliches of the genre: for example, the boat goes over a waterfall but hovers in the air before moving down. After her cartoon character spurns a kiss from the Prince, the real Mary reappears, wearing a highly stereotyped Indian costume complete with huge feather headdress; she is surrounded by dancers in fringed leather outfits. Eventually, the Prince also reappears in a complete cowboy outfit including a huge hat, and they traverse the stage in a canoe as highly exoticized dancers surround them in costumes that combine twenties aesthetics with stereotypical Native American clothing.

In the original production, this number exemplified the revue style, as Frey explains in his Kálmán biography (quotes are from the *Regiebuch*): "For the final 'grand dance arrangement' there even appear 'Indian girls with golden feathers and clothing.' With banjo, saxophone, celeste and exotic percussion, and pentatonic scales, Kálmán represents a fantasy America whose colorful sonority effectively illustrates the visual high point of the operetta" (Frey, 2003, p. 192). This fantasy America, romanticizing both cowboys and Indians, recalls many related works from popular culture, including the 1907 Tin Pan Alley song "Red Wing," a tale of an Indian maiden that is ironically based on Schumann's piano piece "Fröhlicher Landmann" (The Happy Farmer); Karl May's 1893 *Winnetou* trilogy of novels; the song "Indian Love Call" from Rudolf Friml's 1924 operetta *Rose-Marie*; and innumerable Western films. The extravagant live ending in 2004 recalled the staginess and Wild West cliches of the original production, while the animated section paid homage to the first Disney cartoon, "Steamboat Willie," which also debuted in 1928.

This version also represents Bondy as an aspiring film director, expanding the reference to film that comes only at the end of the 1928 version. In the Frey/Wilgenbus adaptation, Bondy often holds a reel of film, sometimes describes his plans for lighting and camera angles, and once even asks the other performers to repeat their lines for a camera retake. Wilgenbus explained that "the aesthetic theme of film was very important in the twenties ... and we considered, we can build that in as a red thread through the story" (Wilgenbus, 2009).

Budapest 2016

In Fall 2017, the Budapest Operetta Theatre and its artistic management agency Pentaton welcomed me to Budapest on several occasions and arranged opportunities to watch performances and conduct interviews. This company works actively to reach out to a public beyond Hungary by arranging international tours and encouraging foreigners to attend their Budapest performances. Their hospitality to me was part of these efforts, reflecting their interest in building a reputation outside the Hungarian-speaking world. Their production of this operetta under its Hungarian title, *A chicagói hercegnö*, was a major success on the Hungarian stage; it also attracted reviews from outside the country. (See e.g. Clarke, 2016 and Ivanoff, 2016.) I include it here because of its importance, though my commentary cannot capture all the details that Hungarian speakers would understand.

As mentioned earlier, this production was inspired partly by the concert version performed by the Komische Oper in Berlin, so it is not surprising that it shares some of Barrie Kosky's approach to operetta. Dramaturg Attila Lőrinczy, who wrote the new dialogue, told me that György Lőrinczy, the director of the company (and Attila's brother) saw the Berlin performance and was impressed by the "basic idea and musical battle" (Lőrinczy, 2017). However, Attila explained that the libretto was "rather idiotic" (*ziemlich blöd*) and that operetta plots in the 1920s and 1930s are not very important. Therefore, the company felt justified in making major changes, and Lőrinczy told me that he changed ninety percent of the dialogue. He defended operetta against intellectuals who see it as old-fashioned; his view is that when the material is exaggeratedly idiotic (*blöd übertrieben*) it can reach the realm of the absurd, nonsensical, and surreal – which makes it much more serious (Lőrinczy, 2017).

Beloved performer Zsuzsa Kalocsai had previously starred in the company's productions of Kálmán's *Csárdásfürstin* and *Gräfin Mariza*, Fall's *Madame Pompadour*, and many other operettas. As one major plot change, the Budapest company designed a new character for her: Grand Duchess Lizaveta of Sylvaria, mother to the Prince (named Boris Alex in their version). She, not the Prince, agrees to sell the castle to Mary. Her son disagrees with that decision and travels to Monte Carlo, where he wins enough money to buy the castle back – and therefore he is absent for most of Act II. As a result, rather than the Prince and Mary becoming closer, it is Mary and the Grand Duchess who develop a mutual appreciation and understanding.

In the Prince's absence, "Rose der Prairie" cannot be used as a romantic duet that brings the couple together. This version preserves only the pentatonic refrain, transformed into an instrumental number played as guests enter the renovated castle for a grand costume ball. This reflects a larger pattern: while many musical numbers from the original *Herzogin* and from other Kálmán shows – *Golden Dawn* (1927) and the operetta film *Ronni* (1931) – are heard, they are often shortened, functioning as brief interruptions of extended comic dialogue rather than presented in full. Music in the Budapest version is often quick and referential, with refrains used as tag lines to identify certain characters, rarely moving into a full number.

The central romantic couple, Mary and Boris Alex, spend little time together. Before his departure for Monte Carlo, they sing the "Armer Prinz" duet – together with a dancer who plays a floppy doll duplicate of the Prince – but Mary performs this number with a scornful expression. In the Vienna production, this number shows Mary's growing empathy for the Prince; in the Budapest production, it remains mocking. Given that approach, and without "Rose der Prairie," there is no real opportunity for Mary and the Prince to be drawn together. When he then returns from Monte Carlo, the added musical number, a romantic waltz duet, has no credible motivation, nor does it make sense that it ends with the couple kissing passionately and tumbling onto a nearby couch for some heavy petting. This unexpected dramatic development emphasizes the convention-bound aspect of operetta, making it completely obvious that these two become a couple only because they are the two main characters. Perhaps this is a deliberate choice, reflecting the absurd and surreal element that Lőrinczy prefers.

With the shift away from romance, other characters gain more prominence. Mary's New York friends appear in added scenes as they visit European capitals and attempt to purchase remarkable possessions there. Mary's personal jazz trio is also a notable presence, often adding a brief riff to spice up the proceedings.

Lonka Kappanyos, junior dramaturg with the Budapest Operetta Theatre, told me that the company must shorten their performances to two acts – though the typical operetta has three, and *Herzogin* four main sections – because much of their audience comes from outside Budapest and needs to leave the theater at a reasonable hour to return home (Kappanyos, 2017). This circumstance may explain the particularly quick and (to me) unsatisfying ending of this version.

After the Prince returns to fling his suitcase of gambling winnings at Mary's feet, the romantic waltz and fondling episode occur, followed by the climax: Mary's friends reveal the contest to the Prince, the Grand Duchess dubs Mary the Duchess of Chicago, and the engagement announcement goes wrong. Boris then starts drinking heavily with his tough-guy friends, leaving the Grand Duchess and Mr. Lloyd to commiserate on the challenges of parenting. During this dialogue, they recognize each other and realize that they were romantically involved decades before. (Lőrinczy told me that the company considered but rejected a tragic ending based on the idea that Mary and Boris Alex are actually half-siblings.) After a tender duet reflecting their outlook as older people, they engineer the required "Happy End" in the final ten minutes. This sudden resolution contributes to the sense of absurdity and satire that Attila Lőrinczy emphasized in our conversation.

Contrasting Moods and Styles

Both these productions were very successful in different ways. The Vienna production was panned by some critics but much appreciated by audiences, and the DVD had good sales. (See Feurzeig, 2016 for more details.) The Budapest production received the award for best production at an annual competition among all Hungarian theaters and became a successful part of the company's strategic effort to draw younger and more fashionable audiences. (Lőrinczy, 2017) While each version was acclaimed, they differ in several ways beyond the plot changes, as explored next.

Representation of Characters

The productions represent the Sylvarian Prince and Morenian Princess in notably different ways. In the original, the Prince displays contrasting character traits: when angry about jazz and American influence, he behaves violently and makes racist and xenophobic remarks, while at other times he has a traditional charm that reflects his courtly upbringing. In the Vienna production, the Prince's more violent side is expressed only in the Grille américaine scene. After that, his rather awkward formality and ceremonial language, while outdated, make him sweetly traditional. (He has a quirk – included in the original libretto – of using the contrasting words "einerseits" and "andererseits" – that is, "on the one hand" and "on the other hand.")

In the Budapest version, the Prince is aggressive and prone to violence. His attendants are not champagne-drinking courtiers, but tough guys who carry big guns and drink large amounts of liquor. Lőrinczy stated that he wrote this character as a "macho Balkan prince" (Lőrinczy, 2017) – perhaps as a way of drawing attention to the fraught situation of the Balkans closer to the present day. The Grand Duke of Morenia, Rosemarie's father, is also gruff and threatening. When the Prince returns toward the end of the show, his macho, violent style is still apparent in his approach to physical intimacy with Mary.[9]

The Viennese Princess Rosemarie is a charming young lady, relatively normal except for being a princess and having a lisp. Her attraction to modern

---

[9] This representation of a tough and violent man attracted to a different kind of woman is reminiscent of the famous 1995 wedding between Arkan, a Serbian warlord, and Ceca, a pop singing star. "Serbia on Sunday celebrated the wedding of its most notorious warlord to its most popular singer at a ceremony where thugs with scars and dark sunglasses rubbed shoulders with pop stars, the spokesman for the ruling Socialists and a senior police chief.... The groom was dressed in a stylized World War I military uniform, his bride wrapped in yards of white tulle in a dress inspired by 'Gone With the Wind.' ... According to tradition, Arkan had to shoot down an apple hanging on a pole above her house. It took six blasts of a twin-barrel hunting rifle. He is, he said, better with a pistol.... No guns, please, guests were forewarned before heading to the church" (Silber, 1995).

innovations is reflected in her interest in jazz and skyscrapers, and she is quite ready to give up her royal position for true love in Chicago. The Budapest Rosemarie has disabilities far beyond a lisp. In Act I, she is portrayed as mentally disabled and very weird. During the formal meeting to finalize the marriage arrangements, the Sylvarian royals and officials are alarmed by her bizarre behavior. Soon after this meeting, Rosemarie meets Bondy and they begin to fall in love. She then obediently opens her arms to be put into a straitjacket before leaving the stage. In Act II she is less peculiar, perhaps tamed or cured by her growing attraction to Bondy, but she remains very childish in her Minnie Mouse costume at the ball.

Contrasts of Costumes and Sets

One important element in this show is the contrast between old European and new American styles, which can be brought out both in costumes and in Mary's renovations to the Sylvarian castle. In the Vienna production, a clear difference in costumes is evident. On the modern American side we have Mary and her flapper friends, who wear slinky knee-length dresses and elegant headdresses that set off their bobbed hair; they also carry long cigarette holders. The dancers for the "American Beethoven foxtrot" wear leotards with feather decorations; their legs are bare and their heads shaved. By contrast, the Prince and his entourage wear military uniforms, providing visual evidence of the traditional hierarchy linked to his kingdom.

The castle in its original decoration is elegantly but sparsely furnished, indicating the financial travails of the monarchy. Mary's renovations include new leather furniture, mechanical conveniences such as a waiter who descends from the ceiling when a button is pushed, and a projected image of skyscrapers lit up at night.

According to Lőrinczy, the Budapest production attempted to be visually bold, representing America in the 1950s–1960s and referencing Pop Art, while showing Sylvaria in about 1900 (Lőrinczy, 2017). Thus the 1920s are not visually present except in some costumes at the costume ball. The Sylvarian castle before the renovation is dark and dingy, decorated with paintings by old masters. After Mary's renovations it is much brighter, and the large central staircase serves as the dramatic entrance for partygoers who wear a wide variety of costumes to represent stereotypes of both America and the Balkans. The selection of characters to represent these cultures is reminiscent of the Hamburg cruise-ship version of *La belle Hélène*. The American stereotypes include athletes, superheroes, women in 1920s clothing, men in business suits, and Mickey and Minnie Mouse (Bondy and Rosemarie). The most notable reference to Balkan stereotypes is a vampire scenario featuring a woman in a long white dress surrounded by frightening-looking men; when they reach the bottom of the stairs, she falls down and the men greedily surround her, apparently attempting to suck her blood.

Musical Contrasts

As Stefan Frey points out, writing about the 1928 production, "The fact that operetta jazz had little to do with real jazz was noticed in Vienna only by the *New York Times* correspondent, since people in Europe knew jazz mostly through the flattened version of the white jazz orchestra à la Paul Whiteman" (Frey, 2003, p. 192). Thus, both versions made adaptations to the musical material to intensify the musical contrasts between jazz and European tradition.

The Volksoper called on Béla Fischer, a highly experienced performer, arranger, and composer in several musical styles including folk music, jazz, rock, and musical theater who has worked on projects with both the Vienna Volksoper and Vienna State Opera. (See Vienna State Opera, Fischer Biography.) The added presence of a jazz pianist was evident at times in the performance. While Wilgenbus and Frey wanted to include a contemporary jazz group onstage to contrast the remarkable Gypsy primás, played by Russian-born violinist Aliosha Biz, this was ruled out for budgetary reasons. (Frey, 2009; Wilgenbus, 2009)

By contrast, the Budapest production was able to include actual jazz, played by an onstage jazz trio led by saxophonist and composer Bálint Bársony. These musicians frequently play when Mary and her American friends are on stage, providing expert jazz improvisation in a post-1920s style that brings more life to the musical presentation. There is also a folk trio representing European traditional music. As Kevin Clarke comments, "at the end the six such different musicians sit playing together, just as Kálmán intended. A great ending both in 1928 Vienna and in Orbán's 2016 Hungary" (Clarke, 2016).

Comparative Reflections

The two main differences between these productions involve the times they represent and their relationship to the original show. The Vienna production focused on the 1920s: that era was reflected in the costumes, the constant presence of film, and the animated sequence during "Rose der Prairie." The resulting show became, at least in part, a meditation on issues of the 1920s – though some of those, particularly the relation between Europe and America, continued to be real and important in 2004.

The Budapest production used two divergent eras as inspiration for costumes and sets, referencing Europe at the turn of the twentieth century and mid century

America. Its presentation of characters in a more caricatured way, including the "macho Balkan prince," the crazy princess, and the stereotypes at the costume ball, created a surreal atmosphere that could be timeless or could equally well reflect on life nowadays in an increasingly absurd and totalitarian Eastern Europe.

The original operetta was set more or less in its own present day, but these revivals, designed over seventy years after the original, could have introduced some interesting anachronisms, capitalizing on that element that was present from the premiere with *La belle Hélène*. This was not a major factor in these productions, though. The Vienna version focused more on the time of the original, emphasizing the media of film and Disney cartoons that were developing then. The Budapest version, while it did include some visuals and jazz styles later than the 1920s, did not present them with the irony we expect from operetta anachronism. The possible exception is its most referential scene, the costume ball, but as a hodge-podge mixture of American and Balkan stereotypes, it did not emphasize temporal incongruity.

In comparison to the 1928 original the Vienna production was a mostly faithful adaptation, while the Budapest version distanced itself much more, almost to the point of using the original as source material from which to create a patchwork quilt. This is reflected in its addition of a character to the story, major plot changes, the use of several Kálmán numbers from other shows – the Vienna production added only one – and the repurposing, shuffling, and condensing of some music for entirely new purposes.

Overall, the Vienna production remained faithful to the Viennese operetta tradition by being bittersweet and sentimental, though not without a good dose of self-aware irony. The Budapest production was more surreal, privileging funny or exciting moments and short-range effects over continuity. The "happy end" is more believable in Vienna; in Budapest, we might expect that not too long after the curtain falls, the American heiress and the Balkan prince will enter into a celebrity divorce worthy of the tabloids.

4 Operetta Revivals and the Rebirth of Satire

In the introduction, we traced the path of operetta from a genre that satirized society to its more nostalgic role in the mid twentieth century. We also observed the decline of operetta, at least in Central Europe, as a living genre with new compositions. First it moved into the revue/jazz operetta style of the late 1920s and 1930s and then it was largely supplanted by the musical – though theater historian Magdolna Jákfalvi does believe that new operettas are being composed today (Jákfalvi, 2017).

For the most part, operetta is now represented in the theatrical world through numerous revivals, including the six productions in the case studies presented in Sections 2 and 3. As we have seen, there is a great deal of creative energy in these highly varied performances. They are exciting, amusing, and appear to be drawing new audiences to operetta. Are they also restoring its earlier function by including social and political commentary? The answer is at least partly "yes." To demonstrate that, here are three examples of cutting political commentary in operetta performances in recent years.

Three Examples

La belle Hélène, *Hamburg 2014*

Toward the end of Act III of *La belle Hélène*, the disguised Paris explains to Menelaus that Helen will need to sacrifice 100 white heifers. Menelaus happily agrees, saying that his people will pay the costs. In the Hamburg production, he gleefully adds the extra line "yes, my children, you will pay." At that moment, the stage darkens and a bent-over woman appears, clearly representing Angela Merkel, chancellor of Germany from 2005 through 2021. She crosses the stage, pushing a wheelbarrow full of Euro bills, while a low brass solo lugubriously plays the opening of Beethoven's "Ode to Joy," anthem of the European Union. In the recorded performance, this entrance was greeted by loud laughter and applause from the audience, at which point the performer paused, set down the wheelbarrow, and bowed while making a vulgar sexual gesture.

This brief addition was an obvious reference to the Greek government-debt crisis of the late 2000s that was solved in 2010 through an EU agreement. Merkel played a leading role, and Germany provided significant money.

> Six years on it is Merkel, not Tusk nor Hollande, who is remembered as the saviour of the euro. Even arch critic Yanis Varoufakis, Greece's former finance minister, told the BBC that Merkel saved the euro by keeping Greece in, although he disagrees with how she did it. The reason is simple: Greece could not have stayed in the eurozone if its largest EU creditor, Germany had not agreed. (Rankin, 2021)

The parallels here are clever. Menelaus's marriage is in trouble. To salvage it, he agrees to finance the sacrifice, but then offloads the cost onto his people. Similarly, in the modern political arena, Greece got into debt but ended up relying on other countries, especially Germany, to cover the bill. The German audience in 2014 clearly appreciated this satirical moment of political reference.

Der Bettelstudent, Vienna 2017

To make sense of the next example, I must explain the genre of the operetta couplet. While there are couplets in French operetta, the tradition of adding improvised verses is particularly linked with Austria: it existed in the *Volkstheater* plays of the early nineteenth century (one classic example is the song "Der Aschenmann" in Ferdinand Raimund's 1827 play *Der Bauer als Millionär*) and was then transferred to operetta.

A couplet is a song with short verses to which the performer adds new improvised verses that refer to current issues, scandals, or gossip. This on-the-spot improvisation was sometimes used to circumvent censorship of the script that had been submitted in advance, and it was especially appealing to spectators, who might attend the same play more than once just to hear the latest couplet stanzas.

In Fall 2017, I attended a performance of Millöcker's operetta *Der Bettelstudent* (The Beggar Student, 1882) at the Vienna Volksoper. This work concerns the Saxon rule of Poland during much of the eighteenth century. The Saxon Colonel Ollendorf has been scorned by a young Polish woman after he kissed her on the shoulder uninvited. Toward the end of Act II, he sings a couplet with the refrain "Schwamm drüber!" That phrase literally means something like "sponge over it" and is used as an expression equivalent to "Forget it" or "Never mind."

In the performance I attended, Ollendorf sang several added stanzas, and an older lady sitting beside me shrieked with delight at one in particular. The chief dramaturg of the Volksoper at that time, Christoph Wagner-Trenkwitz, kindly shared with me the full text of the added stanzas, which he had written. Typically for couplets, they use dialect rather than textbook German (Hochdeutsch). I will quote and summarize here. The first stanza reads as follows:

> Der Schmerz ist ungeheuer,
> Der Brexit, er wird teuer.
> Die Briten ham beschlossen,
> Europa zu verlossen!
> Dass wir sie nicht vergessen,
> schicken sie uns stattdessen
> Charles und Camilla rüber ... Schwamm drüber!
>
> (Wagner-Trenkwitz, 2017)

Roughly translated, this reads: "The pain is monstrous, Brexit is expensive. The Brits have decided to leave Europe. So we won't forget them, they send Charles and Camilla over as a substitute ... Forget it!" The vote approving Brexit had taken place in 2016, and Prince Charles and his wife Camilla had visited Vienna in April 2017, so this was all recent news.

The second stanza concerned a 2016 Austrian scandal in which the designated director of the Staatsoper was accused of plagiarism. The fourth referred to Mother's Day. For me, the third stanza had the greatest impact. It reads:

> Wie wir die Zeit vermissen,
> als man mit Schulterküssen
> die Leute konnt' empören.
> Doch dann gab es zu hören
> des Präsidenten Worte:
> Er greift an andre Orte!
> Obama war uns lieber ... Trump drüber!
>
> (Wagner-Trenkwitz, 2017)

This can be translated as "How we miss the time when one could shock people with shoulder kisses. But then the President's words were heard: he grabs in other places! We liked Obama better ... forget Trump!"

The obvious reference to the "Access Hollywood" tape that was released in 2016 shortly before the election caused my neighbor's appreciative shriek. Donald Trump had recently become President of the United States, and it was particularly interesting for me to hear how he was being satirized in another country. This example, with couplet stanzas referring to Brexit and Trump as a sexual predator, shows that political satire in operetta lives again.

Die Fledermaus, Vienna 2023

In 2022–23, the Volksoper restaged an earlier production of Strauss's *Die Fledermaus*; I attended a performance in June 2023. While the production was not new, the company made a point of emphasizing the casting of a female performer, Sigrid Hauser, as the jailer Frosch. This third-act comedian always has the opportunity to improvise dialogue. Hauser is a renowned singer–actor who has performed on stage, television, and in cabaret.

This act takes place after the huge party at Prince Orlofsky's villa the night before. Prison director Frank returns to his day job after being at the party all night; he is exhausted and extremely drunk. Frosch is also drinking on the job. In this version, the inebriated Frank kept forgetting that a woman had replaced his former male jailer. Frosch took this as an opportunity to make various remarks on gender roles and the need for equal pay. That comment inspired an enthusiastic ovation. To me, the most brilliant part of the dialogue involved her pointing out that frogs (this being the meaning of the name "Frosch") are gender-fluid. It is easy to find confirmation of this: young frogs sometimes change their gender, just as the confused Frank seems to believe has happened to his former employee. While my brief description of this dialogue cannot capture its sharp wit and clever nuances, this was clearly another case when an operetta performance included satirical commentary on current sociopolitical topics.

Summary

From these three examples, it is evident that political references do occur in recent operetta revivals, but not as a consistent element that becomes the main fabric of the presentation. Instead, they appear as isolated jabs, and perhaps they gain their expressive power from their rarity. This is very different from other genres, such as stand-up comedy or late-night television, in which political commentary is a constant. For some audience members, such a moment may become their favorite memory of the show, while others may be more engaged with other materials. As has always been true, operetta is experienced in manifold ways by various spectators.

Other Aspects of Operetta Revival

While there are crystal-clear examples of commentary on current political and social issues in operetta revivals, that is far from the whole picture. Recent operetta productions are moving in various directions of satire, sex, and reinterpretation. Satire is central to the genre, and most original works satirized some aspect of contemporary life. Revivals often shift the satire to emphasize additional topics. Examples include the gentle mockery of Greek tourism in the Paris *Belle Hélène* and the expanded emphasis on American film and cartoon culture in the Vienna *Herzogin*.

Moving the plot to a different era can provide new material to be caricatured. This is true of the Paris and Hamburg *Belle Hélène* productions and the Budapest *Herzogin* production (which combined two eras). The Hamburg production satirized the 1960s by using costumes that referred to brand names, sports teams, and so on, also mocking American mass culture and the fashions of the 1960s, including drug use. This is an expansion on the original anachronism of the operetta, supposedly set in ancient Greece but also satirizing Second Empire France. The Paris and Hamburg productions also framed the story in ways that brought out problems of mid twentieth-century suburban marriage, transferring the Second Empire satire to a more recent (though still past) context.

Early operettas were very open about their sexual content. The mid-century nostalgia and *Heimat* films de-emphasized sex, but it is coming back. This is particularly evident in the Hamburg and Berlin *Hélène* and Budapest *Herzogin* productions: all feature intimate scenes that bring out various approaches to sex, while the Berlin production, with its cross-dressing and naked-buttocks costumes for the male dancers, hints at less conventional sexual practices.

Some operettas create problems through their exoticism, which reflects stereotypes and attitudes of earlier decades. An obvious case is Lehár's *Das Land des Lächelns* (The Land of Smiles, 1929), which examines an intercultural marriage – but in a way that thoroughly stereotypes and largely misrepresents Chinese culture. It also uses simplistic means to represent Chinese music, such as the stereotypical pentatonic scale. While it is difficult to undo this without reorganizing the entire plot, sometimes small steps can be taken. For example, a Vienna Volksoper production in 2009 brought in a troupe of Chinese ribbon dancers, blunting Lehár's musical stereotyping with an authentic dance tradition.

In considering the question of what companies are trying to accomplish these days when they put on a classic operetta in a new form, I see the answer as ranging between two extremes. Some creative teams seem to think that operetta is a type of experience, and their task is to bring that experience to their spectators. At the other end of the spectrum are creative teams who think that an operetta is a specific artwork, and their task is to recreate that work for a new audience.

The "type of experience" approach leads to productions that do not highly respect the materials of the original; thus, they are quite happy to change the story, move around or cut the music, include major interruptions, and add or subtract characters. This approach is most strongly represented by the Berlin and Budapest productions described earlier.

The "recreate a work" approach need not be literal and word-for-word – it is not equivalent to the nostalgic style of earlier decades – but it operates from the assumption that operetta is not purely generic, so the specific characters, plot, thematic content, and musical material of an original work remain central. This is most strongly expressed by the Zurich and Vienna productions described earlier, but I would also place Hamburg and Paris in this camp.

Those working in the "type of experience" style might argue that doing a show in a straight, direct manner is no longer effective, because the original satire has lost its meaning, the plot was idiotic to begin with, and the content and form of operetta must be intensified now in order to achieve a result for modern audiences parallel to its original effect on past audiences.

By contrast, those working in the "recreate a work" approach view the originals as durable and worth preserving. They credit their spectators with the ability to absorb and appreciate that material without adding interruptions or unexpected jolts and thrills for their own sake. Perhaps they are aiming at a different type of audience.

Interestingly, despite the increasing age of the classic operettas – the earliest ones now being nearly 170 years old – many theaters welcome operetta productions representing both approaches, while others such as the Mörbisch Lake Festival emphasize the nostalgic element. It will be interesting to observe which of these styles stands the test of time as the original shows grow older and even more distant from the direct experiences of creative artists and audiences.

Still strongly based on its own genre conventions, including recognizable character types, plot maneuvers, and styles of music and dance, operetta is also regaining its satirical spirit. New productions of old works paradoxically defy many societal conventions through campy mockery of social institutions, direct reference to political controversies, and flagrant representations of sexual experiences and deviance. Perhaps surprisingly, operetta is alive and well. Let us raise a glass of champagne to its future twists, turns, and triumphs!

References

Performance DVDs

La belle Hélène
Staatsoper Hamburg. (2015). C Major Entertainment 730908.
Théâtre Musical de Paris – Châtelet. ArtHaus Musik 107403.
Zurich Opera House. (1997). ZDF/RM Arts 9276RA.
Die Herzogin von Chicago
Volksoper Wien (2004). Capriccio 93509.

Written Sources

Baranello, M. (2021). *The Operetta Empire: Music Theater in Early Twentieth-Century Vienna*, Oakland: University of California Press.

   (2020). The Operetta Factory: Production Systems of Silver-Age Vienna. In A. Belina and D. B. Scott, eds., *The Cambridge Companion to Operetta*. Cambridge: Cambridge University Press, pp. 189–204.

Barbe, A., & Renaud Doucet. (2017). www.barbedoucet.com/about-en.

Belina, A. (2020a). Introduction. In A. Belina and D. B. Scott, eds., *The Cambridge Companion to Operetta*. Cambridge: Cambridge University Press, pp. 1–13.

   (2020b). Operetta in Russia and the USSR. In A. Belina and D. B. Scott, eds., *The Cambridge Companion to Operetta*. Cambridge: Cambridge University Press, pp. 135–48.

   & D. B. Scott, eds. (2020). *The Cambridge Companion to Operetta*, Cambridge: Cambridge University Press.

Bozó, P. (2022). *Offenbach Performance in Budapest, 1920–1956: Orpheus on the Danube*, Cambridge: Cambridge University Press.

Bradley, I. (2005). *Oh Joy! Oh Rapture! The Enduring Phenomenon of Gilbert and Sullivan*, Oxford: Oxford University Press.

Brett, S. (2022). The Mystery of Mari Lwyd. Horniman Museum and Gardens, November 30, 2022. www.horniman.ac.uk/story/the-mystery-of-mari-lwyd/, accessed 5/28/2024.

Clarke, K. (2006). Aspekte der Aufführungspraxis oder: Wie klingt eine historisch informierte Spielweise der Operette? *Frankfurter Zeitschrift für Musikwissenschaft* 9, 21–75. https://bop.unibe.ch/EJM/article/view/6188/8430, accessed 1/18/2025.

(2016). "Die Herzogin von Chicago": Teaching Budapest the Charleston Again. April 23, 2016. http://operetta-research-center.org/die-herzogin-von-chicago-teaching-budapest-charleston-anew/, accessed 5/27/2024.

(2007). *Im Himmel spielt auch schon die Jazzband: Emmerich Kálmán und die transatlantische Operette 1928–1932*, Hamburg: Von Bockel.

Csáky, M. (1998). *Ideologie der Operette und Wiener Moderne: Ein kulturhistorischer Essay*, 2nd revised ed., Vienna: Böhlau Verlag.

Diamond, J. (2012). Where Daisy Buchanan Lived. *The Paris Review*, December 25. www.theparisreview.org/blog/2012/12/25/where-daisy-buchanan-lived/, accessed 5/28/2024.

Dobesch-Warlick, N. (2019). Barrie Kosky on *The Joy of Operetta*. *Bachtrack*, October 2, 2019. https://bachtrack.com/interview-barrie-kosky-operetta-october-2019, accessed 12/26/2024.

Dosch, W. (2020). Franz Lehár und sein Rastelbinder: Operetten-Arisierung und "braune Nachrede." In H. Stockinger and K.-U. Garrels, eds., *"Dein ist mein ganzes Herz": Ein Franz Lehár-Lesebuch*. Vienna: Böhlau Verlag, pp. 89–125.

Driessen, V. M. E. (2023). "The Best from Abroad Is Good Enough for the People of Amsterdam." Operetta Transfer in Amsterdam's Theatrical Landscape, 1860–1880. American Musicological Society conference, Denver, 11 November.

Everett, W. (2024). Personal communication, 7 June.

Feurzeig, L. (2016). Can Creative Interpretation Keep Operetta Alive? Kálmán's *Die Herzogin von Chicago* at the Vienna *Volksoper* in 2004. *Studia Musicologica* 57, 441–70.

(2014). The Queen of Golconda, the Ashman, and the Shepherd on a Rock: Schubert and the Vienna Volkstheater. In C. H. Gibbs and M. Solvik, eds., *Franz Schubert and His World*. Princeton: Princeton University Press, pp. 157–82.

Fraison, L. (1989). Genèse et creation au Théâtre des Variétés. In M. Pazdro, ed., *L'avant-scène: Opéra*, 125, pp. 11–16.

Frey, S. (2020). Going Global: The International Spread of Viennese Silver-Age Operetta. In A. Belina and D. B. Scott, eds., *The Cambridge Companion to Operetta*. Cambridge: Cambridge University Press, pp. 89–102.

(2009). Interview by Lisa Feurzeig in Munich, June 5.

(2003). *"Unter Tränen lachen" Emmerich Kálmán: Eine Operettenbiografie*, Berlin: Henschel.

Green, J. (2025). In a "Show Boat" Reboot, Ol' Man River Gets an Extreme Makeover. *The New York Times*, January 15. www.nytimes.com/2025/01/15/theater/show-boat-under-the-radar.html, accessed 1/19/2025.

Gutknecht, D. (2009). Monteverdi – Mozart – Verdi. Harnoncourt am Opernhaus Zurich. In W. Grätzer, ed., *Ereignis Klangrede: Nikolaus Harnoncourt als Dirigent und Musikdenker*. Freiburg: Rombach, pp. 291–305.

Harnoncourt, N. www.harnoncourt.info/langbiographie/, accessed 6/2/2024.

Ivanoff, A. (2016). An Historically Rich "Duchess of Chicago" in Budapest. May 10, 2016. http://operetta-research-center.org/historically-rich-duchess-chicago-budapest/, accessed 12/23/2024.

Jákfalvi, M. (2017). Interview by Lisa Feurzeig in Budapest, October 27.

Kappanyos, L. (2017). Interview by Lisa Feurzeig in Budapest, October 28.

Kauffmann, M. (2020). Operetta during the Nazi Regime. In A. Belina and D. B. Scott, eds., *The Cambridge Companion to Operetta*. Cambridge: Cambridge University Press, pp. 261–71.

Klotz, V. (2014). *Es lebe: Die Operette. Anläufe, sie neuerlich zu erwecken*, Würzburg: Königshausen & Neumann.

Lőrinczy, A. (2017). Interview by Lisa Feurzeig in Budapest, October 28. (The interview was in German, as this was our common language.)

Lott, F. (2024). Biography. www.felicitylott.de/biography.htm

Meilhac, H., Halévy, L., Capacci, C., Ghesquière, D. and Rissin, D. (1989). *L'avant-scène opéra* 125 (November 1989): Offenbach: *La belle Hélène*. In M. Pazdro, ed., *L'avant-scène: Opéra*, Paris: L'Avant-Scène.

Milford, N. (1970). *Zelda: A Biography*, New York: Harper and Row.

Minkowski, M. Biography. marcminkowski.com/biography, accessed 1/12/2025.

Müller, U. (2014). "*Regietheater*/Director's Theater." In H. M. Greenwald, ed., *The Oxford Handbook of Opera*. New York: Oxford University Press, pp. 582–605.

Neuschäfer, H.-J. (1985). Die Mythenparodie in *La belle Hélène*. In W. Kirsch and R. Dietrich, eds., *Jacques Offenbach, Komponist und Weltbürger: Ein Symposion in Offenbach am Main*. Mainz: Schott, pp. 111–26.

Preston, R. (2021). Love, Murder, Mob Justice: Reimagined Musical "Oklahoma!" Is Finally Coming to Minneapolis. *Minneapolis Star Tribune*, November 8. www.startribune.com/groundbreaking-chestnut-oklahoma-has-been-reimagined-for-21st-century/600114104, accessed 1/19.2025.

Rankin, J. (2021). The Crisis Manager: Angela Merkel's Double-Edged European Legacy. *The Guardian*, September 23, 2021. www.theguardian.com/world/2021/sep/23/the-crisis-manager-angela-merkels-double-edged-european-legacy, accessed 1/18/2025.

Rhinwedd. (2024). The Story of Mari Lwyd. https://rhinwedd.cymru/blogs/news/the-story-of-marilwyd#:~:text=Thought%20to%20have%20originated%20from,and%20Joseph%20to%20have%20shelter, accessed 5/28/2024.

Rissin, D. (1989). Commentaire musicale et littéraire. In M. Pazdro, ed., *L'avant-scène: Opéra*, Paris: L'Avant-Scène.

Schmid, R. (2014). In Berlin, "Hélène" Not So Belle and "Tosca" is Teutonic. *Classical Voice North America: Journal of the Music Critics Association of North America* (October 17, 2014). https://classicalvoiceamerica.org/2014/10/17/berlin-komische-opera-la-belle-helene-not-so-belle-and-staatsoper-tosca-is-teutonic/, accessed 06/02/2024.

Schneider, H. (2020). Metamorphosen der *belle Hélène* von Meilhac, Halévy und Offenbach – Meilhac's, Halévy's, and Offenbach's Metamorphoses of *La belle Hélène*. *Archiv für Musikwissenschaft* 77, 23–48.

Scott, D. B. (2020). Operetta Films. In A. Belina and D. B. Scott, eds., *The Cambridge Companion to Operetta*. Cambridge: Cambridge University Press, pp. 272–85.

Senelick, L. (2017). *Jacques Offenbach and the Making of Modern Culture*, Cambridge: Cambridge University Press.

Silber, L. (1995). Serb Warlord's Truly Shotgun Wedding: Matrimony: Weapons Blazing, a Suspected War Criminal also Wanted by Interpol marries the Queen of "turbo-folk" Music. *Los Angeles Times*, February 20, 1995. www.latimes.com/archives/la-xpm-1995-02-20-mn-34114-story.html, accessed 5/26/2024.

Stephinson, A. (2023). Design Wizard Jean-Charles de Castelbajac Reflects on His Pop-Inspired Collaborations with Andy Warhol and Keith Haring. *Artnet*, January 20, 2023. https://news.artnet.com/art-world/jean-charles-de-castelbajac-maison-et-objet-2244610, accessed 2/17/2024.

Sullivan, J. (2017). Boston New Wave Band Human Sexual Response Promises to Reunite in "Fabulous" Style, WBUR Radio, October 31, 2017. www.wbur.org/news/2017/10/31/human-sexual-response, accessed 1/18/2025.

Vienna State Opera. Biography of Béla Fischer. www.wiener-staatsoper.at/en/staatsballett/compagnie-leadingteams/team/biografien/bela-fischer/, accessed 5/26/2024.

Wagner-Trenkwitz, C. (2017). Added text for couplets in Millöcker's *Der Bettelstudent*, personal communication.

  (2022). *Willkommen, Bienvenue, Welcome! Musical an der Volksoper Wien*, Vienna: Amalthea.

Wilgenbus, D. (2009). Interview by Lisa Feurzeig in Munich, June 6.

Yon, J.-C. (2007). L'opérette antique au XIXe siècle: un genre en soi? In *Figures de l'Antiquité dans l'opéra français: des Troyens de Berlioz à OEdipe d'Enesco: Actes du Colloque du IXe Festival Massenet, Saint-Étienne, 9 et 10 novembre 2007*, 127.

Acknowledgments

I am deeply grateful to so many people who made this work possible. Most of them are listed below; any omissions are entirely accidental.

When I began this work in 2009, the Vienna Volksoper staff sent me reviews and arranged interviews; thanks to them and to those who spoke with me in Vienna and elsewhere, including performers Mehrzad Montazeri and Norine Burgess (near Toronto); directors Dominik Wilgenbus and Stefan Frey (in Munich); intendant Rudolf Berger; and authorities on Austrian culture Waltraud Heindl, Hanna Bubeniček, Morten Solvik, and Erich Neuwirth. Special gratitude to the whole Neuwirth family, who have become my Austrian family over the years.

My Vienna stay in 2017–18 was made possible by the IFK International Research Center for Cultural Studies and the Fulbright Scholar Program. Special thanks to IFK director Thomas Macho and the institute's incredibly supportive staff, especially Petra Radecki, Julia Boog-Kaminski, and Daniela Losenicky, and also to the Austria Fulbright Office, particularly Lonnie Johnson and Susanne Hamscha. Other IFK Fellows and Fulbright Scholars enriched my intellectual and personal life that semester, including Rositza Alexandrova, Ana de Almeida, Jesse Feiman, Joseph Malherek, Alexander Honold, Birgit Mersmann, and Thomas Prendergast. Love and thanks to Rudi Pietsch, the sadly missed founder and leader of the Tanzgeiger, for his insight into operetta's connections to folk dance.

At the Volksoper, chief dramaturg Christoph Wagner-Trenkwitz passed on his deep knowledge of theater and operetta in many conversations, shared interesting documents, and gave permission for me to attend rehearsals of Benatzky's *Axel an der Himmelstür* and Heuberger's *Der Opernball*. I deeply appreciate the warmth and welcome I received from many performers, including Wolfgang Gratschmaier, Kurt Schreibmayer, and Ursula Pfitzner, and from archivist Felix Brachetka. Scholar Hans-Dieter Roser also met with me and shared his insights. Our landlords, Karin and Josef Steiner, were tremendously hospitable and helpful during our months living in Vienna, and the First Vienna Bilingual Middle School, directed by Frau Martha Hafner, welcomed and taught our daughter.

I visited Budapest three times to attend performances of the Budapest Operetta Theatre. Many thanks to the Pentaton agency which set up those visits, particularly András Szentpéteri and Nóra Czvikli, who provided free tickets, scheduled interviews, and recommended lodging. Much appreciation to those who spoke with me: dramaturg Attila Lőrinczy, junior dramaturg Lonka Kappanyos, and theater historian Magdolna Jákfalvi – and also to Lonka and Magdolna for a delightful trip to see Kálmán's *Csárdáskirálynö* in Kecskemét! For further help comprehending the Hungarian operetta world, I am grateful to my old friends Lynn Hooker, Kati Szvorák, and Tamás Repiszky for their deep knowledge of Hungarian culture. And much appreciation to the staff at the charming Hotel Ambra.

My interactions with the Komische Oper in Berlin were brief, as I was only able to be there for one weekend. Thanks to dramaturg Johanna Wall for meeting with me to discuss the Berlin production of *Die schöne Helena*, and later to Theresa Rose and Trevor John Pichanick for their help in sending a DVD performance to me in Michigan on loan.

My colleagues at Grand Valley State University helped in many ways. Thanks and appreciation to dance costumer Cat O'Callaghan and theatre professors James Bell and Alli Metz for sharing their knowledge. John Schuster-Craig, who had just retired, returned to teach my classes for the month of January 2018 while I was still in Austria. Department chair Danny Phipps and the Dean's Office for the College of Liberal Arts and Sciences supported my research and helped make the travel possible.

Derek Scott, renowned scholar of popular music, advocated for this work when it was still quite new and organized conferences where I could share it with others, including William (Bill) Everett, editor of this series. I deeply appreciate Bill's encouragement when I had doubts about this project and his patience when it took much longer than originally planned. Operetta expert Kevin Clarke shared his knowledge and enthusiasm for the genre, and collectors Mike and Nan Miller shared the *Herzogin* Regiebuch with me. Peter Laki (the musicologist, not the operetta singer) performed Kálmán's "Rose der Prairie" with me in Hermann, Missouri – practically on the banks of the Missouri River, where the song is set.

My family uprooted their lives to make this research possible. It is not easy to leave home for almost six months at age thirteen, so my daughter April deserves special recognition, along with my beloved partner, John Sienicki, for supporting both of us.

Cambridge Elements

Musical Theatre

William A. Everett
University of Missouri-Kansas City

William A. Everett, PhD is Curators' Distinguished Professor of Musicology at the University of Missouri-Kansas City Conservatory, where he teaches courses ranging from medieval music to contemporary musical theatre. His publications include monographs on operetta composers Sigmund Romberg and Rudolf Friml and a history of the Kansas City Philharmonic Orchestra. He is contributing co-editor of the *Cambridge Companion to the Musical* and the *Palgrave Handbook of Musical Theatre Producers*. Current research topics include race, ethnicity and the musical and London musical theatre during the 1890s.

About the Series

Elements in Musical Theatre focus on either some sort of "journey" and its resulting dialogue or on theoretical issues. Since many musicals follow a quest model (a character goes in search of something), the idea of a journey aligns closely to a core narrative in musical theatre. Journeys can be, for example, geographic (across bodies of water or land masses), temporal (setting musicals in a different time period than the time of its creation), generic (from one genre to another), or personal (characters in search of some sort of fulfilment). Theoretical issues may include topics relevant to the emerging scholarship on musical theatre from a global perspective and can address social, cultural, analytical and aesthetic perspectives.

Cambridge Elements =

Musical Theatre

Elements in the Series

A Huge Revolution of Theatrical Commerce: Walter Mocchi and the Italian Musical Theatre Business in South America
Matteo Paoletti

The Empire at the Opéra: Theatre, Power and Music in Second Empire Paris
Mark Everist

"Why Aren't They Talking?": The Sung-Through Musical from the 1980s to the 2010s
Alex Bádue

Offenbach Performance in Budapest, 1920–1956: Orpheus on the Danube
Péter Bozó

West Side Story in Spain: The Transcultural Adaptation of an Iconic American Show
Paul R. Laird and Gonzalo Fernández Monte

Kickstarting Italian Opera in the Andes: The 1840s and the First Opera Companies
José Manuel Izquierdo König

Singing Zarzuela, 1896–1958: Approaching Portamento and Musical Expression through Historical Recordings
Eva Moreda Rodríguez

The Revue in Twentieth-Century Budapest: From Cosmopolitan Nightclubs to Stalinist Dogma
Dániel Molnár

Gypsy *and the Broadway Musical Madwoman: A Feminist Analysis*
Mary Beth Sheehy

The Rebirth of Satire in Revivals of European Operettas
Lisa Feurzeig

A full series listing is available at: www.cambridge.org/EIMT

For EU product safety concerns, contact us at Calle de José Abascal, 56–1°, 28003 Madrid, Spain or eugpsr@cambridge.org.

www.ingramcontent.com/pod-product-compliance
Ingram Content Group UK Ltd.
Pitfield, Milton Keynes, MK11 3LW, UK
UKHW020839200625
459861UK00016B/258